COMFORT FOOD COOKBOOK

Comfort Food Feel With the Healthy Food Benefits

(Classical Comfort Foods From American Kitchens)

Zoe Brown

Published by Alex Howard

© **Zoe Brown**

All Rights Reserved

Comfort Food Cookbook: Comfort Food Feel With the Healthy Food Benefits (Classical Comfort Foods From American Kitchens)

ISBN 978-1-990169-58-8

All rights reserved. No part of this guide may be reproduced in any form without permission in writing from the publisher except in the case of brief quotations embodied in critical articles or reviews.

Legal & Disclaimer

The information contained in this book is not designed to replace or take the place of any form of medicine or professional medical advice. The information in this book has been provided for educational and entertainment purposes only.

The information contained in this book has been compiled from sources deemed reliable, and it is accurate to the best of the Author's knowledge; however, the Author cannot guarantee its accuracy and validity and cannot be held liable for any errors or omissions. Changes are periodically made to this book. You must consult your doctor or get professional medical advice before using any of the suggested remedies, techniques, or information in this book.

Table of contents

Part 1 1
Introduction 2
Barbeque Burger 4
Lasagna All Daiya Long 6
Mighty Mac And Cheese 9
Blue Cheese Buffalo Wings 11
Meatball Mania 13
Meatbella Subs 15
Pizza Pie In A Pan 18
Rice Wine Ramen 20
Green Bean Cassoyrole 23
Makes: 4 To 6 Servings 23
Wham Bam Clam Chowder 25
Cumin, Cilantro And Chili, Oh My! 27
A Vegetable Stew To Root For 29
Lentil Just In Thyme Soup 31
Maki Me Mouth Water 33
Seitan Shish Kebabs 36
Custom Crab Cakes 39
No Whey! It's Tofu Omelettes 41
Yummus Hummus 44
No, Shiitake, It's Bacon! 46
When Jelly Met Muffins 47
Spinach Skinny Dip 49

Guaca Whacka Mole 51

Three C Black Forest Cake 52

If That Doesn't Take The Chocolate Cake! 56

Applesauce Cake 60

A Chocolate Chip Cookie By Any Other Name 62

Rolling In Cookie Dough 64

Cinnamon Rolls To Make Your Eyes Glaze 66

Mini Nutmeg Donuts 69

No Kidding! Breakfast Pudding! 71

Nothin' Better Than Brownies 72

Captivating Cupcakes 74

Part 2 76

Introduction 77

Breakfast 81

Cheesy Tomato Stuffed Waffles 81

Spicy Italian Sausage Patty With Mexican Cheese Dip 82

Mediterranean Style Polenta Stack 85

Vegan Omelet 87

Main Dishes 88

Vegetable & Cheesy Rice Bake 88

Italian Wonder Pot 89

Vegetable Lasagna Recipe 91

Cheesy Rice Casserole 95

Grilled Spicy Cheese Shashlik 97

Quesadilla- Spicy Tortillas Filled With Cheesy Vegetables 99

Baked Vegan Cheesy Crisps 101

Cheesy Broccoli Tots With Cheddar Onion Sauce 102

Cheesy Vegetable Burgers 104

Cheesy Onion Grilled Sandwich... 105

Mozarella Bread Pizza... 108

Grape And Maple Syrup Cream Cheese Crostini..................... 111

Southwestern Grilled Vegan Cheese Sandwich 112

Dinner... 113

Vegan Margherita Pizzas... 113

Vegan Stuffed Shells 116

Classic Baked Macaroni And Cheese 118

Broccoli Shells N' Cheese 119

Cream Cheese Mashed Potato.. 121

Desserts.. 122

Raw Vegan Cheesecake 122

Chocolate-"Cheesecake" Bars With Pine Nuts........................ 124

Cherry Cheesecake Cookies 126

Frosted Cream Cheese Butternut Cookies............................. 129

Creamy Vegan Garlic Pasta With Roasted Tomatoes.............. 132

Creamy Butternut Squash Linguine 134

Creamy Avocado Pasta 136

Vegan Meatloaf 137

Baked Squash 139

Caesar Salad 141

Vegan Cobb Salad 143

Veggie Dogs... 145

Eggplant Parmesan With Cashew Ricotta.............................. 147

Lasagna With Basil Cashew Cheese 150
Lentil Steaks With Mushroom Gravy 152
Vegan Carbonara 154
Vegan Tortilla Soup 156
Mushroom Bean Avocado Toast 158
Roasted Cauliflowers With Tomato Sauce 160
Tofu Cashew Coconut Curry 162
Vegan Frittata 164
Spinach Ravioli 166
Peanut Noodles 167
Creamy Vegan Pasta 169
Taco Pizza 171
Vegan Chili Cheese Fries 173
Saucy Meatballs With Spaghetti 176
Chickpea Curry With Potatoes 179
Classic Vegan Coleslaw 181
Herbed Potato, Asparagus And Chickpeas 183
Banana Chia Pudding 185
Creamy Broccoli Cheese Soup 187
Grilled Cheese With Smoky Tomato Soup 189
French Dip Sandwiches 191

Part 1

Introduction

If you're a Vegan, you're certainly not alone, though sometimes it might feel that way.

Three percent of American adults – 7.3 million people – follow a vegetarian diet, and one million of those vegetarians are vegans, who eat no animal products at all — no meat, fish, eggs, milk, cheese, even honey.

Having been born, raised, and grew up in the Midwest, two dietary staples for this part of the country are meat and dairy. Admittedly, the thought of being a Vegan and choosing not to eat meat and dairy seems a lot like choosing not to breathe air. However, as time has moved forward and more people I know have chosen to eat Vegan, I can now better comprehend just how difficult it has been for my family and friends across the country who choose to live their lifestyle in a meat and dairy society.

Being a Vegan is incredibly challenging whether its physical or social or economic in nature. Giving up favorite foods is tough enough and the fact that family and friends are unsympathetic and unsupportive only compounds the challenge and – in some cases – isolation from the meat and dairy eaters. The lack of social support is frustrating, disappointing, and isolating. Many non-Vegans don't understand and don't want to. Not eating meat and dairy is a foreign concept. It's weird. It's not natural. Vegans are mocked, looked down upon, and condescended to and it makes the effort of staying true to one's belief even more difficult.

Vegan cooking at home? Vegan ingredients and cooking techniques can be overwhelming. Recipes in most cookbooks are tough to make with non-dairy substitutes that can leave one with a most unsatisfying taste. The challenges of cooking and baking for the Vegan extend to something meat and dairy eaters take for granted – comfort foods. Easy enough for a non-Vegan to grab or prepare a comfort food. But if you're a Vegan and crave a burger, lasagna, mac and cheese, or really any dessert, what are you to do?

That's why I selected and compiled this book full of recipes. In these pages you'll find classic American comfort foods for Vegans that are tasty and easy to prepare.

Enjoy!

Barbeque Burger

Makes: 5-6 patties

Ingredients

1/2 cup cooked brown rice, short grain
1/2 - 3/4 cups whole peanuts, roasted & salted (process until crumbly bits)
1 cup mashed sweet potato (oven baked)
1 1/2 cups cannellini white beans, drained/rinsed in hot water to soften
1 Tbsp dry BBQ spice blend
2 Tbsp liquid BBQ sauce, vegan
1/4 cup onion, diced
2 Tbsp flat leaf parsley, finely chopped
1/4 tsp fine black pepper
salt to taste

Other ingredients:

oil for sauteing (optional)
burger buns, vegan
vegan mayo
sliced avocado (tossed in lemon juice)
slaw (optional topping or side)
toppings: onion, tomato, mixed greens
warmed BBQ sauce

Directions:

1. Preheat oven to 400 degrees.
2. Prep: prep your veggies, process your peanuts and cook your rice. I used my Vitamix to process my peanuts. You want a blend of fine crumbles that range from powdery to chunky.

3. Combine your sweet potato, rice, beans, peanuts, spices, onion, parsley and BBQ sauce in a large mixing bowl. Start mashing! Mash until the mixture is thick and creamy.
4. Spray a baking sheet with oil - must do to prevent sticking. Bake at 400 degrees for about 15 minutes or until edges brown. I like my patties on the softer side so I always under cook them a bit. If sauteing, add a splash of safflower or extra virgin olive oil to a hot sautepan and cook 2-4 minutes on each side over medium-high heat. Patties will fuse and firm up a bit as they cool.
5. Assemble: Toast buns. Slather warmed BBQ sauce on one bun and vegan mayo on the other. Place patty. Add onions, tomato, sliced avocado and greens.

Lasagna All Daiya Long

First, you'll need to make the Basil Cashew Cheeze Sauce:

Ingredients:

¼ cup vegetable broth or water (or more as needed)

¼ cup fresh lemon juice

½ cup nutritional yeast

(Nutritional yeast is a deactivated yeast, which is sold in the form of flakes or as a yellow powder similar in texture to cornmeal. You can find it at health food stores or you can order it online.)

¾-1 tsp kosher salt (or to taste) plus freshly ground black pepper
1 Tbsp Dijon mustard
2 garlic cloves, peeled
1½ cups fresh basil leaves (lightly packed)
1 cup raw cashews, soaked in water for 30 minutes or overnight

STEP 1:

Drain and rinse the soaked cashews. Add all ingredients (in the order listed) to a high-powered blender, such as a Vitamix, and blend until smooth.

YIELDS (1) 9 x 13 PAN OF LASAGNA

Ingredients:

½ Tbsp extra-virgin olive oil
3 garlic cloves, minced
1 sweet onion, chopped
2 zucchini, chopped

8 oz. package of sliced baby bella mushrooms

1 large or 2 small red peppers, chopped
1 large handful of spinach
Herbamare or salt/pepper to taste
1½ jars of pasta sauce or homemade marinara sauce
1 box of oven-ready lasagna noodles (no boiling required)
Lemon Basil Cheeze Sauce (from above)
1½ cups Cheddar and/or Mozzarella Style Daiya Shreds

STEP 1:

Preheat oven to 400°F. In a large skillet, add oil, onion and garlic; sauté over low-medium heat for 5 minutes. Add zucchini, mushrooms, peppers; sauté for 10 more minutes. Add spinach; sauté for 5 more minutes. IMPORTANT: Season well with Herbamare or salt and black pepper or else you'll have bland vegetables.

STEP 2:

Pour about a cup or so of pasta sauce into a 9×13 pan and spread it evenly. Add a layer of noodles, then half the Lemon Basil Cheeze Sauce, then half the vegetables (sorry, forgot to snap a photo of that layer).

STEP 3:

Repeat layers of pasta sauce, noodles, cheeze sauce, veggies. Add another layer of pasta sauce, then sprinkle Daiya Shreds on top.

STEP 4:

Cover with foil and slice a few small vents using a sharp knife. Bake for 40-45 minutes. Remove foil and broil for 5 minutes on medium, watching closely so as not to burn the edges.

Mighty Mac And Cheese

Makes: 6 servings

Ingredients:

4 quarts water

1 Tbsp sea salt 8 ounces macaroni (gf if needed, I recommend quinoa pasta)

4 slices of bread, torn into large pieces (gf if needed or use pre-made gf breadcrumbs)

2 Tbsp non-hydrogenated vegan margarine (such as Earth Balance, which is also gf)

¼ tsp paprika

Sauce Ingredients:

2 Tbsp shallots, peeled and chopped

1 cup red or yellow potatoes, peeled and chopped

¼ cup carrots, peeled and chopped N cup onion, peeled and chopped

1 cup water ¼ cup raw cashews 2 tsp sea salt ¼ tsp garlic, minced N cup non-hydrogenated vegan margarine (such as Earth Balance, which is also gf)

¼ tsp Dijon mustard 1 tsp lemon juice, freshly squeezed ¼ tsp black pepper J

tsp cayenne

STEP 1: In a large pot, bring 4 quarts water and 1 tablespoon sea salt to a boil. Add macaroni and cook until al dente. In a colander, drain pasta and rinse with cold water. Set aside.

STEP 2: In a food processor, make breadcrumbs by pulverizing the bread and 2 tablespoons margarine to a medium-fine texture. Set aside.

STEP 3: Preheat oven to 350°F. In a saucepan, add shallots, potatoes, carrots, onion, and 1 cup water; bring to a boil. Cover the pan and simmer for 15 minutes, or until vegetables are very soft. Do not drain vegetables.

STEP 4: In a blender, process the cashews, salt, garlic, N cup margarine, mustard, lemon juice, black pepper and cayenne. Add softened vegetables and cooking water to the blender; process until perfectly smooth.

STEP 5: In a large bowl, toss the cooked pasta and blended cheese sauce until completely coated. Spread mixture into a 9 x 12 casserole dish (86L: I used 9 x 9, which worked perfectly), sprinkle with prepared breadcrumbs, and dust with paprika. Bake for 30 minutes or until the cheese sauce is bubbling and the top has turned golden brown.

Blue Cheese Buffalo Wings

Start with the Buffalo Bites first, then make the dressing while the bites are baking.

SERVES 4

INGREDIENTS FOR BUFFALO BITES:

1 cup water or soy milk (I used 1/2 cup of each)
1 cup flour (any kind of flour will work – even gluten-free!)
2 tsp. garlic powder
1 head of cauliflower, chopped into bite-size pieces
1 cup buffalo or hot sauce (Be sure to check the ingredients in the buffalo/hot sauce – not all are vegan.)
1 Tbsp. olive oil or melted vegan margarine

STEP 1
Preheat oven to 450°.

Combine the water and/or soy milk, flour and garlic powder in a bowl and mix well.

STEP 2
Grease a shallow baking dish/pan (I used two small ones) with cooking spray or vegetable oil.

Dip each piece of cauliflower into the flour mixture, let the excess drip off and place it in the greased baking dish. As you can see in my photo, I didn't let the excess drip off well enough. I had to cut off the rubbery batter spills from some of the pieces after they cooked.

STEP 3
Bake for 20-25 minutes.

While this is baking, make the blue cheese dressing (see recipe further below).

STEP 4
Mix the buffalo sauce and olive oil or vegan margarine in a small bowl (I used a Pyrex 2-cup measuring cup).

STEP 5
Pour the hot sauce mixture over the baked cauliflower and continue baking for another 5 to 8 minutes.

Serve with Vegan Blue Cheese Dressing (recipe below) and celery sticks.

INGREDIENTS FOR VEGAN BLUE CHEESE DRESSING:

1/4 block of firm or extra firm tofu

dash of garlic powder
1 cup of vegan mayonnaise

1/4 tsp. tahini (sesame seed paste)

fresh lemon juice
apple cider vinegar

STEP 1
(I forgot to photograph this step). In a medium size bowl, mix all ingredients except the tofu. Mix until it has a nice, smooth consistency.

STEP 2
Crumble tofu. This will be the 'lumps' in your dressing. Add tofu to dressing mixture and stir until combined.

Meatball Mania

Preparation time: 15 minute(s)
Cooking time: 20 minute(s)
Number of servings: **6 (about 12 balls)**

These balls are similar to falafel in texture, and because they are bean and grain based, they will fall apart if submerged in sauce for too long. So it's best to add them to your sauce briefly after it's hot or pour the sauce over them.

Ingredients

- 1/3 cup chopped walnuts (1.5 ounce), or other nuts or seeds (see notes below)

- 1/3 cup rolled oats (quick or old fashioned) or quinoa flakes

- 1/2 cup chickpea flour (besan)

- 1/4 cup kasha (gluten-free) or bulgur wheat (not gluten-free), fine or medium granulation

- 1 tablespoon potato or corn starch

- 1 tablespoon nutritional yeast

- 2 teaspoons dehydrated onion flakes

- 1 teaspoon dried oregano

- 1/2 teaspoon dried basil

- 1/2 teaspoon granulated garlic

- 1/2 teaspoon smoked paprika

- 1/2 teaspoon baking soda
- 1/2 teaspoon salt
- 1 teaspoon tomato powder, optional
- 1/2 teaspoon fennel seeds, optional
- 1/2 teaspoon red pepper flakes, optional

Instructions

1. Put the nuts and oats (or quinoa flakes) into a food processor and pulse several times to coarsely chop the nuts. Do not grind to a flour–they should be about the size of popcorn kernels. Pour into a bowl or storage bag.
2. Add all remaining ingredients and mix well. Keep prepared mix in the refrigerator until ready to use.
3. To make the entire batch of mix, pour it into a bowl and add 2/3 cup boiling water. Stir and let stand for 15 minutes as you preheat oven to 350 F.
4. Using wet hands, form the mixture into about 12 1-inch balls. Place on a silicone mat or oiled baking sheet. Bake for 20-25 minutes, turning once halfway through. Cover with hot spaghetti sauce and serve.
5. To make 1/2 a batch, measure out 3/4 of a cup of the mixture and add 1/3 cup boiling water. Proceed as above.

Note

To keep these gluten-free, be sure to use gluten-free oats or quinoa flakes. Not all people following a gluten-free diet can tolerate oats, so ask first.

Meatbella Subs

Makes: 12 "meatballs" & veggie filling for 2 subs

Ingredients:

For the walnut bella "meatballs"

1 cup walnuts*
   *For a nut-free version use pepitas (raw hulled pumpkin seeds)

4oz baby bella mushrooms - cut in half

1tsp all-purpose savory seasoning

4 sprigs fresh parsley

4 medjool dates- pitted

1/2 tsp salt

1 tsp olive oil

1 cup fresh bread crumbs (1 slice of bread)

1 flax egg (1 tbsp ground flax & 3tbsp warm water, mixed and set aside for 5 minutes)

For the veggie filling

1/2 orange bell pepper sliced into strips
1 cup grape tomatoes cut in half
1/2 large shallot sliced
1 tsp olive oil
pinch of salt
2 tbsp balsamic vinegar
2 sub rolls toasted

parsley for garnish

Assembly:

1. Preheat oven to 400*

2. Finely grind the slice of bread into crumbs in a food processor - transfer crumbs to a small bowl & set aside.

3. In the food processor, finely ground 1 cup walnuts, half of the mushrooms, seasoning & parsley until well mixed. the mixture should be a bit moist from the walnuts. transfer mixture to a medium mixing bowl.

4. Add dates and remaining mushrooms to the processor until well ground. with a rubber spatula transfer date/mushroom mixture to the bowl with the walnut mixture. add bread crumbs, olive oil, salt and flax egg - mix well.

5. A heaping tablespoon at a time form a ball with the mixture - place on a parchment lined baking sheet. continue 12 times until all the mixture has been formed into balls.

6. Bake for 15-20 minutes until brown.
7. While the "meatballs" are baking - prep your veggies.
8. In a medium saute pan over medium/high heat - add oil, once oil is heated add veggies and saute. caramelized bits are good. Toward the last 2-3 minutes of cooking, add the balsamic to de glaze the pan. Continue to cook until balsamic is reduced to 1/2 - you are looking to create a glaze of balsamic on the veggies. Remove from heat and set aside.

9. When you have about 2-3 minutes of cooking time left on the "meatballs" place 2 sub rolls cut side down on the upper rack of the oven.

10. Once the "meatballs" are done cooking, remove from the oven along with the sub rolls. Allow the "meatballs" to cool for about 3 minutes.

11. Assemble the subs by placing half the veggie mixture into the roll, top with walnut bella "meatballs" and garnish with parsley

12. Leftover "meatballs" can be stored in an airtight container for up to week and reheated as needed or frozen on a cookie sheet and stored in a freezer bag for later use.

Pizza Pie In A Pan

Serves: 6

Ingredients:

1 homemade or prepared pie crust
3 cups assorted heirloom tomatoes - sliced
1 small /medium eggplant, thinly sliced & salted
2 cloves of garlic
olive oil
salt & pepper
handful of fresh basil - torn

Directions:

1. Pre heat oven to 425

2. Line a tart pan with parchment paper

3. Thinly slice eggplant and spread out on a paper towel, salt well on both sides, cover with another paper towel and allow to sit and drain while you prep the tomatoes

4. Slice the tomatoes to your desired thickness

5. Chop the garlic

6. Remove pie crust from the fridge and press into the tart pan. Layer the bottom of the tart with the eggplant, then the tomatoes on top of the eggplant in any pattern that you wish, overlapping of the tomatoes is fine.

7. Sprinkle the garlic over the tomatoes.

8.   Drizzle with olive oil and sprinkle with a good amount of flaky salt & freshly cracked pepper.

9. Bake in the pre heated oven at 425 for 20 minutes, reduce oven temp to 375 and continue baking for an additional 20 minutes.

10. Remove from oven and allow to cool. Sprinkle with torn basil just before serving.

Rice Wine Ramen

Total time: 3 hours (or overnight)
Active time: **30 minutes**

Serves: 4 to 6

Note: You definitely want the right noodles for this! A trip to an Asian grocery should provide you with a wall of ramen to choose from. If you can't find the right kind of noodles anywhere, then any supermarket should have those packaged noodles, and there is often a vegan flavor.

Ingredients:

8 oz plain ramen noodles
1 recipe Miso Dashi Broth

For the marinade:
1/2 cup hoisin sauce
1 tablespoon soy sauce or tamari
3 Tablespoons rice wine vinegar
1 tablespoon brown sugar
1 tablespoon fresh lime juice

For marinating:
12 to 14 oz block extra firm tofu, pressed
1/4 lb shiitake mushroom, rough stems trimmed

For the bok choy:
4 baby bok choy sliced in half
2 tablespoons toasted sesame oil
1/2 teaspoon salt

For garnish:
1 ripe avocado, diced small
1 cup thinly sliced scallion

Directions:

1. In a wide shallow bowl, mix together all of the marinade ingredients.

2. Slice tofu into 8 even slabs widthwise. Place in marinade for at least 2 hours and up to overnight, flipping occasionally.

3. Keep the shiitake mushrooms on standby, as they will be dredged in the marinade prior to grilling.

4. When the tofu has marinated, cook the noodles according to package directions, then immediately cool them under cold running water, and set aside. Also, make sure your broth is piping hot and ready to go, since everything else will happen rather quickly.

5. Heat up a grill to about 450 F.

6. We're going to put the bok choy on the grill first. Brush each half with sesame oil, and sprinkle with a little salt. Place face down on the grill for about 5 minutes, until grill marks appear. Keep the leaves away from the direct flame, if possible, since they will burn if too close to the fire. As you can see, I keep one half of the grill off, so that the leaves don't burn.

7. Brush the grill with a little sesame oil, and place the tofu on the grill as well, cooking along with the bok choy for about 5 minutes. Once the tofu is on the grill, dredge the mushrooms in the marinade.

8. When you remove the bok choy, flip the tofu, to grill for another 5 minutes. Use a thin metal spatula to flip, so that you can really get under the tofu and it doesn't stick. In the meantime, place the dredged mushrooms on the grill, and let them grill for 5 minutes as well.

9. Now remove the tofu and mushrooms from the grill. It's time to assemble your ramen!

10. Place the cooked noodles in the hot broth to heat through, just for about 30 seconds. Divide into big bowls.

11. Slice tofu slabs on a bias, and divide amongst the bowls. Add bok choy, mushrooms and and avocado in little piles. Scatter scallion across the top, and serve immediately!

Green Bean Cassoyrole

Makes: **4 To 6 Servings**

Ingredients:

1/2 medium onion, diced
3/4 cup chopped button mushrooms
1 Tbsp. vegetable oil
1/2 tsp. oregano
1/2 tsp. thyme
1/2 tsp. sage
Salt and pepper, to taste
1 1/2 cups unsweetened soy milk
1 cube vegetarian bouillon
2 1/2 Tbsp. cornstarch
2 Tbsp. cold water
1 can cut green beans
1 6-oz. can French-fried onions

Directions:

1. Preheat the oven to 350°F.

2. Sauté the onions and mushrooms in the vegetable oil in a skillet. Add the herbs, salt, and pepper.

3. Heat the soy milk and bouillon in a saucepan, stirring until the bouillon dissolves. Do not bring to a boil. Mix together the cornstarch and water and add to the pan, stirring well.

4. Quickly add the green beans, the sautéed veggies, and about half of the French-fried onions and stir well.

5.Pour the mixture into a casserole dish and top with the remaining French-fried onions.

6.Bake for about 15 minutes, or until the onions begin to brown.

Wham Bam Clam Chowder

Serves: 4

Ingredients

¾ cup water
1 cup soy creamer, plain
1 cup soy milk, plain

splash of truffle oil (white or black)
1 tsp extra virgin olive oil
½ tsp salt
¼ tsp fine black pepper
spices of your choice
⅓ cup nutritional yeast
1 medium potato, peeled, boiled and cut into quarters
⅓ cup white onion, cut into large chunks
1¾ cup raw cashews, soaked overnight in salted water

MUSHROOM "CLAM" SAUTÉ:

2 tsp safflower oil

3-4 king oyster mushrooms, cubed 1/4" thick
1 cup celery, chopped
½ cup white onion, diced
splash of liquid smoke
splash of truffle oil
a few dashes of salt (or seasoned salt)

STEP 1:

If you forgot or don't have time to soak your cashews overnight, an alternate method is to simmer cashews over medium heat in salted water for 25 minutes. Either way, drain and rinse cashews. Add all of the ingredients (except the Mushroom "Clam" Sauté ingredients) to a high speed blender, such as a Vitamix. Add liquids first, then spices, then soft ingredients, then firm ingredients. If you don't have a high-speed, heavy-duty blender, you may want to split the ingredients in half and do two batches. Start on low and slowly increase speed until the cashews are puréed and the mixture is creamy. You can add more liquid if you prefer a thinner soup. Taste soup and adjust seasonings as needed. Pour soup into a sauce pan over low heat.

STEP 2:

Heat safflower oil over medium-high heat. Add celery, onion and mushrooms to pan; sauté over high heat for about 2 minutes. Season lightly with salt. Add a splash of truffle oil and liquid smoke halfway through the cooking process.

STEP 3:

Add most of the mushroom mixture to the sauce pan with the soup. Reserve some of the mixture for garnish. Stir the soup and continue to heat until warmed through. Serve in soup bowls or in bread bowls, if you like. Garnish with reserved "clam" mixture.

Cumin, Cilantro And Chili, Oh My!

Total Time: 45 minutes
Makes: 6 to 8 servings

Ingredients

1 tablespoon vegetable oil

1 onion, medium dice

1 carrot, medium dice

2 garlic cloves, minced

Kosher salt

Freshly ground black pepper

1 bell pepper, medium dice

1 zucchini, medium dice

2 teaspoons ground cumin

2 tablespoons plus 1 teaspoon chili powder

2 (15-ounce) cans light kidney, dark kidney, or black beans, drained and rinsed

1 1/2 cups water

1 (28-ounce) can chopped tomatoes

Chopped cilantro, for garnish

Quartered lime pieces, for garnish

Directions

1. Heat the oil in a large heavy-bottomed pot with a tightfitting lid or a Dutch oven over medium heat until shimmering. Add the onions, carrots, and garlic and season with salt and pepper.

Cook, stirring occasionally, until the onions have softened, about 5 minutes.

2.Add the bell pepper and zucchini to the pot and season with salt and pepper. Add the cumin and chili powder and stir to incorporate. Cook, stirring occasionally, until the carrots are knife tender, about 8 to 10 minutes.

3.Add the beans, water, and tomatoes with their juices and stir to combine. Increase the heat to high and bring to a boil. Reduce the heat to low and gently simmer until the vegetables are soft and the flavors have melded, about 15 minutes. Taste and season with additional salt and pepper if necessary. Serve and garnish as desired.

A Vegetable Stew To Root For

Total Time: 30 minutes, plus 3 1/2 hours cooking time
Makes: 6 to 8 servings

Ingredients

1/4 cup olive oil

2 medium yellow onions, large dice

Kosher salt

1 1/4 teaspoons ground ginger

1 (3-inch) cinnamon stick

1/2 teaspoon ground coriander

1/4 teaspoon ground cumin

1/8 teaspoon cayenne pepper

Pinch saffron threads

Freshly ground black pepper

1 pound Yukon Gold potatoes (about 3 large), large dice

1 pound carrots (about 4 to 5 medium), peeled and large dice

1 pound parsnips (about 4 medium), peeled and large dice

3 cups low-sodium chicken or vegetable broth

2 pounds sugar baby pumpkin or butternut squash (about 1 small), peeled, seeded, and large dice

1 pound sweet potatoes (about 2 medium), peeled and large dice

1 (15-ounce) can chickpeas, also known as garbanzo beans, drained and rinsed (about 1 1/2 cups)

1/2 cup golden raisins, also known as sultanas

1 bunch spinach, trimmed and washed (about 4 cups loosely packed)

1 1/2 tablespoons cider vinegar, plus more as needed

Directions

1. Heat the oil in a large frying pan over medium heat until shimmering. Add the onions and a pinch of salt and cook over medium heat until translucent, about 4 minutes. Add the ginger, cinnamon, coriander, cumin, cayenne, saffron, and a pinch of pepper and cook until fragrant, about 1 minute.

2.Transfer the mixture to a slow cooker, add the potatoes, carrots, parsnips, and broth, season with salt and pepper, and stir to combine. Cover and cook on high for 1 1/2 hours.

3.Add the pumpkin or squash, sweet potatoes, chickpeas, and raisins, season with salt, and stir to combine. Cover and continue to cook on high until a knife easily pierces the vegetables, about 2 hours more, stirring after 1 hour. Add the spinach and gently mix (do not overmix). Let sit until wilted. Gently stir in the vinegar, taste, and season with more salt, pepper, and vinegar as needed.

Lentil Just In Thyme Soup

Total Time: 1 hour
Makes: 6 servings

Ingredients

1 tablespoon olive oil

1 medium celery stalk, small dice
1 medium carrot, peeled and small dice
1/2 medium yellow onion, small dice
3 medium garlic cloves, minced
Kosher salt
Freshly ground black pepper
1 quart low-sodium vegetable broth
1 (15-ounce) can diced tomatoes with their juices
1 1/4 cups lentils (any color except red), rinsed
1 bay leaf
1/4 teaspoon finely chopped fresh thyme leaves
1 teaspoon red wine vinegar or sherry vinegar
2 ounces spinach leaves (about 1/2 a bunch)

Directions

1. Heat the oil in a large saucepan over medium heat until shimmering, about 3 minutes. Add the celery, carrot, and onion and cook, stirring occasionally, until the vegetables have softened, about 10 minutes. Stir in the garlic and cook until

fragrant, about 1 minute. Season with several generous pinches of salt and pepper.

2.Add the broth, tomatoes with their juices, lentils, bay leaf, and thyme and stir to combine. Cover and bring to a simmer, about 15 minutes. Once simmering, reduce the heat to low and continue simmering, covered, until the lentils and vegetables are soft, about 15 minutes more.

3.Taste and season with more salt or pepper as needed, then stir in the vinegar. Add the spinach and stir until wilted. If you prefer a creamier texture, purée half of the soup in a blender and add it back to the pot.

Maki Me Mouth Water

Makes: 36 rolls

Ingredients:

3 nori sheets cut in half
(6 half sheets)
1 avocado, skin removed & thinly sliced
1/2 sweet potato, peeled and cut into matchsticks
1 cup sushi rice (dry)
prepared according to directions on the box
1 tbsp black sesame seeds
1 tbsp sesame seeds

If frying sweet potato

1/2 cup panko bread crumbs
1 tsp sesame oil
1 tbsp vegetable oil
1 flax egg: 1 tbsp ground flax plus 3 tbsp warm water

For the eel sauce/Japanese Tsume

1/4 cup mirin
1/4 cup tamari
1/4 cup granulated sugar
pickled ginger, tamari & wasabi for serving

Assembly:

1. Wrap your sushi mat in plastic or a large ziploc bag- set aside

2. Prepare sushi rice according to package (this can be done in advance)

3. Steam peeled sweet potato matchsticks until tender; about 15 minutes

4. If frying, heat oils in a medium saute pan over medium high heat

5. Coat sweet potato sticks in flax egg, then in panko

6. Transfer to the frying pan and cook until golden brown on each side

7. Transfer to a plate lined with a paper towel and allow to cool to the touch

To make the sushi

1. Cut each sheet of nori in half lengthwise

2. Working with one sheet at a time place shiny side down onto your covered sushi mat

3. With about a 1/2 cup of sushi rice spread onto nori leaving about 1/2 inch space at the top; sprinkle with sesame seeds

4. Flip rice covered nori so the uncovered edge is closest to you

5. Place a single layer of sweet potato & avocado about halfway up the nori roll with sushi mat

6. With a sharp knife slice in half then each half into 3 pieces

7. Move to a serving plate and repeat until all nori is used

To make the eel sauce:

1. In a small sauce pot over medium heat combine all ingredients

2. Whisk until sugar is dissolved

3. Continue to cook over medium/low heat (gentle simmer) until sauce thickens

4. Sauce will continue to thicken as it cools, remove from heat just at the point before desired thickness is achieved

5. Drizzle eel sauce over sushi

6. Serve with tamari, pickled ginger & wasabi

Seitan Shish Kebabs

Total active time: about 1 hour
Total passive time: 45 minutes, to simmer the seitan
Yields: about 7-8 cups

Ingredients

For the seitan*

1 cup vital wheat gluten
1/4 cup whole wheat pastry flour
1/2 cup chickpea flour (reduce to 1/4 cup if pan-frying instead)
1 cup cold vegetable broth
2 TB dark sesame oil
1 TB white or chickpea miso
1 TB fermented black bean sauce
*the seitan may be made, simmered and stored in the broth until ready to grill.

For the simmering broth

6 cups cold vegetable broth
several cloves of garlic, smashed
2 TB soy sauce
2 TB raw agave
1 cup of ice cubes

For the marinade

1 cup brown sugar
1 cup rice vinegar
2/3 cup sambal oelek
1/2 cup sriracha

2 TB vegan Worcestershire Sauce
1 TB grated ginger

Directions

To make the seitan, combine the flours together. Then, in a separate bowl, whisk together the rest of the seitan ingredients, then add it to the flour mixture. Knead in a Kitchen Aid mixer using the dough hook attachment or knead with your hands for one minute to form a cohesive ball of dough. Tear off small, jagged skewer-sized pieces and place to the side. (The pieces will double in size during simmering time.)

To make the simmering broth, combine the broth, garlic, soy sauce, agave and ice cubes in a medium-sized pot. Do not turn on the heat yet—you want the broth to be very cold when you add the seitan to it.

Next, place enough olive oil to cover the bottom of a cast iron pan or any other non-stick pan. Heat the oil over medium heat. Place the seitan chunks in the pan and allow to brown on both sides. Transfer to a plate to cool.

Drop the cooled seitan chunks into the broth. Bring to a very small simmer, then maintain that heat for about 45 minutes. Cover with a lid that allows some steam to escape during cooking time. Do not allow the broth to boil at any time—it will affect the texture, making it spongy.

To make the marinade, add all of the marinade ingredients in a saucepan. Toss the seitan chunks in the marinade, then thread onto metal or wood skewers. (If you are using wood skewers, soak them in water first for about an hour to prevent them from burning.)

Now bring the leftover marinade to a small boil in a small saucepan, reduce the heat, and allow to simmer and thicken for 7-10 minutes.

Grill the seitan, turning and basting often with the reduced marinade. Serve immediately, drizzling any extra sauce over the top.

Custom Crab Cakes

Ingredients

For the crab cakes

1 cup of farro
3 cups broth
1/4 cup shallots, minced
1 sheet of toasted nori, crushed into a powder
1 tsp Old Bay seasoning
1 tsp dried dill
1-2 tsp sriracha
2 tsp capers, plus 2 tsp of the brine
8 Ritz crackers, crushed with your fingers
1 1/2 tsp Ener-G, whisked with 2 TB water
1 tsp baking powder
1 1/2 TB raw tahini
1/4 cup chopped red or orange bell pepper
1/3 cup panko crumbs, for breading
cooking spray, or olive oil, for frying

For serving

1/8 cup each of sriracha and Vegenaise, for serving OR 1 tsp dried dill, mixed with 1/3 cup Vegenaise

Method

To prepare the farro, rinse it in a sieve, then transfer to a medium-sized pot. Add the three cups of broth, bring to a boil, then cover and reduce to a low simmer for about 25 minutes. Check the farro after 20 minutes—it should be slightly chewy and expanded to twice its size. Continue to simmer for an additional 5 minutes if needed, then drain any extra broth off the farro and allow it to cool.

Transfer the farro to a food processor and pulse just a few times—you still want it to be a little chunky. Remove it from the food processor and place it into a medium-sized bowl.

Next, transfer the rest of the crab cake ingredients into the food processor, except for the bell pepper, and pulse until combined, then transfer it into the bowl with the farro.

Fold in the bell pepper and stir to combine. Then, place the mixture in the refrigerator to chill for at least an hour.

When you are ready to make the crab cakes, divide the mixture in half, then form six equal portions from each half to create 12 equal-sized portions. Roll them into balls, then flatten them out between your palms a bit. Press them into the panko crumbs, tapping off any extra.

Heat a skillet over medium heat. Add about a tablespoon of olive oil or some cooking spray into the pan, then fry the cakes until golden brown. Serve immediately with the sriracha or dill sauce.

No Whey! It's Tofu Omelettes

Time: 30 minutes
Active time: **30 minutes**

Makes: 4 omelets

Ingredients

2 cloves garlic (optional)
1 14 oz package silken tofu, lightly drained (not the vacuum packed kind), or soft tofu (see tip)
2 tablespoons nutritional yeast
2 tablespoons olive oil
1/2 teaspoon turmeric
1 teaspoon fine black salt, plus extra for sprinkling
1/2 cup chickpea flour
1 tablespoon arrowroot or cornstarch

Directions

1. Chop up the garlic up in a food processor. Add the tofu, nutritional yeast, olive oil, turmeric and salt. Puree until smooth. Add the chickpea flour and cornstarch and puree again for about 10 seconds, until combined. Make sure to scrape down the sides so that everything is well incorporated.

2.Preheat a large, heavy bottomed, non-stick skillet over medium-high heat. Well-seasoned cast iron works great, but if you're not sure of the non-stickness of your cast iron, do a test (see tip above) or use a regular non-stick skillet. Lightly grease with either cooking spray or a very thin layer of oil. (The less oil the better for the nice brown speckles we're going for.) Also, make sure that you use a large skillet, as you need room to spread out the omelet and to get your spatula under there to flip. Don't use an 8- inch omelet pan. Here you'll need at least 12 inches.

3.In 1/2 cup measurements, pour omelet batter into skillet. Use the back of a spoon or a rubber spatula to spread the batter out into about 6- inch circles. Be gentle when spreading it out, if there are any rips or holes, that is fine, just gently fill them in as you spread the batter. Let cook for about 3 to 5 minutes before flipping. The top of the omelet should dry and become a dull matte yellow when ready to flip. If you begin to flip it and it seems like it might fall apart, give it a little more time. When the omelet is ready to be flipped, the underside should be flecked with light to dark brown when it is ready to flip. Flip omelet and cook for about a minute on the other side. Keep warm on a plate covered with tin foil as you make the remaining omelets.

4.Stuff omelet with the fillings of your choice then fold over. Once the omelet has been filled, sprinkle with a little extra black salt, since some of its flavor disappears when cooked.

Fillings options:

When it comes to omelet fillings, think fresh and you can't go wrong. Hit up your farmer's market and go with what's in season. Each of these fillings makes enough for 4 four omelets. Mix and match them to your heart's content and come up with scrumptious fillings of your own.

Mushrooms And Spinach

Preheat a large pan over medium heat. Sautée 4 cups sliced cremini mushrooms in 2 tablespoons olive oil. After about 5 minutes, when mushrooms are soft, add 2 cloves minced garlic and about 3 tablespoons fresh chopped thyme. Sautée about 3 minutes more, add fresh black pepper and a few dashes of salt to taste. Stuff into omelets and divide 2 cups of fresh, chopped spinach amongst them. The spinach will wilt in the omelet. Top with homemade cheezy sauce or shredded vegan cheese and fold.

Roasted Tomatoes, Ricotta And Basil

Preheat an oven to 300° F. Slice 2 pounds of plum tomatoes lengthwise. Toss with 2 tablespoons olive oil. Sprinkle with salt and fresh black pepper. Place tomatoes face down on a rimmed baking sheet and roast for about an hour and a half. Stuff omelet with Cashew Rriccotta and about 10 leaves fresh basil for each, then add tomatoes and fold.

Sausage And Peppers

Preheat a large pan over medium high heat. Saute 4 sliced sausages and 2 medium diced red peppers in 2 tablespoons olive oil. Stuff into omelets and, if you like, top with homemade cheezy sauce or shredded vegan cheese and fold.

Yummus Hummus

Preparation time: 10 minutes
Cooking (blending) time: **2 minutes**

Number of servings (yield): **6**

Ingredients

1/3 cup cashews

1 1/2 cups cooked, drained chickpeas, divided
3 ounces silken tofu (1/4 package MoriNu brand)
6 tablespoons pimentos (about 4 ounces), drained well, divided
3 tablespoons nutritional yeast
2 tablespoons lemon juice
2 cloves garlic
1 teaspoon spicy brown mustard
1/2 teaspoon granulated onion
1/2 teaspoon smoked paprika
1/4 teaspoon cayenne (red) pepper (or to taste)
1 teaspoon salt, or to taste (use less if chickpeas are salted)

Instructions

1. Place the cashews in a small bowl and cover them with water.

Allow them to soak at least 2 hours and up to overnight.

2. Drain the cashews. Put half of them into the food processor along with half of the chickpeas, the silken tofu, 4 tablespoons pimentos, and all remaining ingredients. Process until it's as smooth as you can get it. Then add the remaining cashews and

chickpeas and pulse about 10 times until chickpeas and cashews are broken but not completely smooth.

3.Check seasonings and add more red pepper and salt to taste. Transfer into a serving bowl and stir in the remaining 2 tablespoons of pimentos. Refrigerate for at least an hour to allow flavors to blend.

For a soy-free option, try using a couple of tablespoons of almond or rice milk instead of the silken tofu.

No, Shiitake, It's Bacon!

Ingredients

1 TB olive oil
1/4 tsp salt
3/4 tsp liquid smoke
1 tsp sesame oil
2 cups shiitake mushroom caps, sliced thinly

Method

Preheat oven to 350. Place a silpat over a baking sheet, set aside.

Combine all of the ingredients except for the sliced shiitake into a shallow glass pyrex or bowl. Whisk to combine.

Add in the sliced shiitake, and stir gently to combine. Allow to marinate for 20 minutes to an hour.

Place the shiitake in a single layer onto the silpat. Bake for 10 minutes, flip, then bake for an additional 15 minutes. Increase the heat to 375, then bake for 10 minutes more. Flip, then finish for 10 more minutes. Keep an eye on them towards the end to ensure they do not burn.

Remove from the oven and place on paper towels to drain. As they drain, the edges will become crispy. Serve immediately.

Baking times will differ based on the thickness and type of shiitake you are using. After baking for 15-20 minutes, just keep an eye on them to prevent burning.

When Jelly Met Muffins

Total Time: About 50 minutes
Makes: 12 muffins

Special equipment: Be sure to use standard (2-1/2-inch diameter) muffin liners. If you bake these without liners, the jelly will leak out and stick to the pan.

Ingredients

1 1/2 cups all-purpose flour

3/4 teaspoon baking powder

1/2 teaspoon baking soda

1/2 teaspoon ground nutmeg

1/2 teaspoon fine salt

1 cup plain soy or rice milk

1 teaspoon cider vinegar

2 tablespoons cornstarch

3/4 cup plus 2 tablespoons granulated sugar

1/3 cup vegetable oil

2 teaspoons vanilla extract

1/3 cup raspberry, strawberry, or grape jam or preserves

Powdered sugar, for dusting

Instructions

1. Heat the oven to 350°F and arrange a rack in the middle. Line a 12-well (1/2 cup) muffin pan with paper liners; set aside.

2. Sift the flour, baking powder, baking soda, nutmeg, and salt into a large bowl. Make a well in the center of the mixture; set aside.

3. In a medium, nonreactive bowl, whisk together the soy or rice milk, vinegar, and cornstarch until the cornstarch has dissolved. Pour this into the well in the flour mixture. Add the granulated sugar, oil, and vanilla and stir with a rubber spatula until combined (there will be a few lumps).

4. Fill each muffin well about three-quarters full. Using a spoon, create a small indentation in the batter by slightly spreading it from the middle out toward the edges. Measure 1 heaping teaspoon of jam or preserves and place the back of the teaspoon inside the indentation. Rotate the spoon, letting the jam slide into the indentation. Repeat in each well.

5. Bake until the tops of the muffins are firm, about 21 to 23 minutes. Set the pan on a wire rack and let cool for 5 minutes. Remove the muffins from the pan and let cool completely on the wire rack. Dust with powdered sugar before serving.

Jelly doughnuts meet berry muffins in these subtly sweet vegan morning pastries. Choose whichever jam strikes your fancy for the filling, or try adding some chocolate or mashed bananas.

Spinach Skinny Dip

Ingredients

¾ cup plain unsweetened almond milk

2½-3 tbsp freshly squeezed lemon juice

1-2 medium-large cloves garlic
¾ tsp sea salt
½ tsp dry (ground) mustard
freshly ground black pepper to taste
¾ cup raw cashews (unsoaked)
2 cups frozen artichoke hearts, partially thawed
2 cups (loosely packed) spinach leaves

STEP 1:

Preheat oven to 425ºF. In a blender, add milk, lemon juice, garlic, salt, dry mustard, pepper and cashews. Blend until very smooth. If using a Vitamix or other high-powered blender, this will only take a minute or so. If using a standard blender, keep blending until very smooth.

STEP 2:

Add artichokes and spinach and very briefly blend or pulse. Do not fully blend, keep some chunky texture! My mixture wasn't quite as chunky as I prefer, so I scooped the mixture into a bowl and stirred in a can of quartered artichoke hearts (drained, rinsed and chopped).

STEP 3:

Transfer mixture to an oven-proof baking dish, and bake for 17-20 minutes. Do not bake any longer or the spinach will turn off-color.

Serve warm with raw veggies, bread, tortilla chips, pita bread/chips or crackers. I liked it even better after letting it cool, then refrigerating and re-heating it later.

Guaca Whacka Mole

Total Time: 10 minutes
Active Time: 10 minutes
Makes: About 6 cups

Ingredients

9 large avocados (about 3 pounds) Look for avocados that give slightly when pressed but are not completely soft.

1 medium Roma tomato (about 1/4 pound), finely chopped

1/4 cup finely chopped cilantro

2 tablespoons thinly sliced scallions

1 to 2 medium serrano chiles, seeded and minced

1/4 cup freshly squeezed lime juice

1 tablespoon kosher salt

Directions

1. Halve the avocados, remove the pits, and scoop the flesh into a large mixing bowl. Mash with the back of a large fork or a potato masher to make a chunky paste.

2. Add the remaining ingredients and stir to combine. Taste, adjust the seasoning as needed, and serve immediately.

Three C Black Forest Cake

Makes: 6 to 8 servings.

For the Chocolate Génoise:

Non-stick cooking spray
200 g (1 cup) evaporated cane juice (granulated sugar)
75 g (1/3 cup) nondairy butter (or use 1/3 cup vegetable oil, no need to cream with sugar)
1 teaspoon pure vanilla extract
1/2 teaspoon pure almond extract
1 teaspoon cornstarch
190 g (1 1/2 cups) all-purpose flour
40 g (1/2 cup) unsweetened cocoa powder (or use 20 g unsweetened cocoa powder and 20 g Dutch-process cocoa powder)
1 tablespoon baking powder
1 cup nondairy milk

For the Chantilly filling:

1 container (1 pound) refrigerated Healthy Top
2 tablespoons amaretto (or regular) agave nectar
1 teaspoon pure vanilla extract
A few drops pure almond extract

For dipping the Génoise:

1 1/2 cups cooled black cherry tea (or regular black tea), steeped from at least 2 teabags
2 teaspoons to 1 tablespoon Kirschwasser, optional

For the Cherries:

10 vegan maraschino cherries, patted dry (be sure they're pitted and stemmed) OR reconstitute 10 dried cherries by soaking them in 1/4 cup hot water with a few drops pure almond extract until they plump up, about 15 minutes, then drain and pat dry

For decoration purposes:

1. Frozen dark chocolate bar to shave right on top of the cake.

2. To make the génoise: Preheat oven to 350°F (180°C, or gas mark 4). Lightly coat a 9 x 13-inch (23 x 33-cm) baking pan with spray. Using an electric mixer, cream together sugar, butter, extracts and cornstarch.

3. In a separate large bowl, sift together flour, cocoa, and baking powder.

4. Add dry ingredients to wet, along with milk, and stir just until combined and smooth.

5. Place batter into prepared pan, and spread it evenly with an offset spatula.

6. Bake for 25 minutes. Let cool in pan for 10 minutes. Carefully flip over a cooling rack, let cool completely.

7. Once cooled, cut into 24 lady finger strips/skinny bars. Be gentle, as the génoise will be fragile.

8. Preheat oven to 350°F (180°C, or gas mark 4) again. Carefully place all the bars on a cookie sheet lined with parchment paper or a silicone baking mat. Bake for another 15 minutes. Place on a cooling rack to cool completely.

Chantilly Filling

1. In the meantime, make the Chantilly filling: Whip all ingredients together using a handheld mixer in a large bowl for about 3 minutes, until fluffy.

Important: Keep a little less than 1/2 cup of it on the side, in the fridge, to put a touch of decoration to the finished product.

2. Use a 10 x 7-inch (25 x 18-cm) ceramic dish to assemble the dessert, but an 8-inch (20-cm) square dish would be fine too.

3. Stir the optional Kirschwasser into the cooled tea. Place into a shallow dish. Briefly and carefully dip each fragile génoise bar into the tea, letting the excess liquid drip back into the shallow dish. Cover the bottom of the pan/dish with half (12) of the génoise bars.

4. Use half of the Chantilly filling, and plop it onto the layer of génoise bars, carefully spreading it evenly with an offset spatula. Randomly and lightly press cherries into the Chantilly filling. Dip each of the (12) remaining génoise bars into the cooled tea (again, letting the excess drip off), and cover the Chantilly filling with them.

5. Use the remaining Chantilly filling to cover the second layer of génoise bars, carefully spreading it evenly with an offset spatula.

6. Refrigerate for at least 3 hours or overnight. Give the whole dish at least 1 hour in the fridge before covering it with plastic wrap, so that the Chantilly doesn't adhere to the wrap. Don't forget to cover and place the remaining Chantilly filling back into the fridge, too.

Eating

When the time finally comes to partake, there are various ways to serve this:

1. Cover the whole thing with chocolate sprinkles you will use a potato peeler or a chef's knife to shave off a frozen dark chocolate bar, decorating the cake with the remaining Chantilly, using a pastry bag and the tip of your choice. Scoop out portions into dessert dishes. It's a little less good-looking than what follows, but it does the trick.

2.For a cleaner portioning, you could do what I did up there and use a 3-inch deep, 4-inch wide plastic cutter to get 2 pretty servings from the middle of the pan (it takes some wiggling and careful prodding to plate it, but if my clumsy hands can do it, so can yours) and scoop what remains in bowls. Decorate with chocolate shavings and Chantilly clouds. Note that placing the cutters into the dish and then freezing it all for 1 hour makes it easier to transfer. Just be sure to give it some fridge time to thaw out a little once plated.

3.Or you could also make individual servings in pretty dessert dishes by doing the layering in there directly: no transferring involved, far less mess and less headaches.

If That Doesn't Take The Chocolate Cake!

Total Time: 1 hour, plus baking and cooling time
Makes: 1 double-layer 9-inch cake (10 to 12 servings)

Ingredients

For the cake:

2 cups all-purpose flour, plus more for coating the pans

2/3 cup natural unsweetened cocoa powder

2 teaspoons baking powder

1 teaspoon baking soda

1/2 teaspoon fine salt

2 ounces natural unsweetened chocolate, finely chopped (about 1/4 cup)

2 cups plain, unsweetened soy or rice milk

2 teaspoons cider vinegar

2 sticks (8 ounces) unsalted, nonhydrogenated margarine, at room temperature, plus more for coating the pans

1 cup packed dark brown sugar

2/3 cup granulated sugar

1 tablespoon vanilla extract

For the frosting:

1 pound vegan bittersweet chocolate, finely chopped (about 3 1/4 cups)

4 sticks (1 pound) unsalted nonhydrogenated margarine, at room temperature

2 2/3 cups powdered sugar, sifted

1/4 teaspoon fine salt

1/2 cup natural unsweetened cocoa powder
6 tablespoons soy or rice milk
1 tablespoon vanilla extract

Directions

For the cake:

1. Heat the oven to 350°F and arrange a rack in the middle. Coat 2 (9-inch) round cake pans generously with margarine. Line the bottom of each pan with a round of parchment or waxed paper, then coat the paper with more margarine. Dust the pans all over with flour, tapping any excess out; set aside.

2. Sift the measured flour, cocoa powder, baking powder, baking soda, and salt into a medium bowl; set aside.

3. Using a microwave or double boiler, melt the chocolate in a small bowl; set aside to cool slightly. In a medium, nonreactive bowl, combine the soy or rice milk and vinegar; set aside.

4. In the bowl of a stand mixer fitted with a paddle attachment, beat the margarine and sugars on medium-high speed until fluffy and well combined, about 3 minutes, stopping as needed to scrape down the sides of the bowl. With the mixer on medium speed, add the melted chocolate and vanilla and beat until just combined. Scrape down the sides of the bowl. Reduce the speed to low, add a third of the flour mixture, and mix until just incorporated. Add a third of the soy milk mixture and mix until just incorporated. Continue with the remaining flour and soy milk mixtures, alternating between each and stopping to scrape down the sides of the bowl as needed, until all ingredients are just incorporated.

5.Divide the batter between the prepared pans and spread the tops evenly with a spoon or spatula. Bake until a toothpick inserted into the center comes out clean, about 30 to 35 minutes.

6.Remove from the oven and let the cakes cool in their pans on a rack for 10 minutes. Slide a thin paring knife around the edges, invert the cakes onto the rack, remove the bottom round of paper, and cool completely.

For the frosting:

1. Using a microwave or double boiler, melt the chocolate in a medium bowl; set aside to cool.

2.In the bowl of a stand mixer fitted with a paddle attachment, beat the margarine on medium-high speed until fluffy, about 2 minutes, stopping to scrape down the sides of the bowl. Turn the mixer to low, add the sugar and salt, and mix until incorporated. Increase the speed to medium high and beat until fluffy, about 3 minutes, stopping to scrape down the sides of the bowl.

3.With the mixer on low, gradually add the cooled melted chocolate and beat until incorporated. Stop the mixer and add the cocoa powder, soy or rice milk, and vanilla. Beat on low until incorporated, then beat on medium high until the frosting is airy and thoroughly mixed, about 1 minute, stopping once to scrape down the sides of the bowl.

To assemble:

1. Transfer one of the cake layers, bottom side up, to a serving plate, 9-inch cardboard round, or cake stand. Spoon a third of

the frosting into the center of the cake layer. Work an offset spatula or wide butter knife in a gentle swirling motion and spread the icing into an even layer from the center toward the edges of the cake (if you need to add more icing, add it to the center and work it out toward the sides).

2.Carefully set the second cake layer on top of the first, bottom side up. Evenly spread another third of the frosting over the top and sides of the whole cake. (Don't worry about looks at this point—this is just a thin basecoat, a.k.a. a crumb layer, and it will be covered up later.) Place the cake in the refrigerator until the frosting on the outside is slightly hard, about 15 minutes.

3.Remove from the refrigerator and evenly spread the remaining frosting over the top and sides of the cake.

Applesauce Cake

Yield: 8 slices or more

Ingredients

210 g whole wheat pastry flour
1/2 teaspoon fine sea salt
1/2 teaspoon nutmeg
1/2 teaspoon cinnamon
1/2 teaspoon allspice
140 g organic powdered sugar
1 1/2 teaspoons baking powder
1 tablespoon Ener-g egg replacer powder
8 ounces applesauce
1/2 cup olive oil
1/4 cup water
Vegan whipped topping, quantity to taste

Directions

1. Preheat oven to 350°F (180°C, or gas mark 4). Lightly coat an 8-inch cast iron skillet or baking pan with non-stick spray.

2. Sift the flour, salt, spices, sugar, baking powder and egg replacer powder in a large bowl.

3. Whisk applesauce, oil, water until combined.

4. Stir wet ingredients into dry, being careful not to over mix.

5. Place into prepared pan and bake for 30 to 35 minutes, or until a toothpick inserted in the center of the cake comes out clean.

6.Transfer onto a wire rack to cool completely before topping with whipped cream.

A Chocolate Chip Cookie By Any Other Name…

Total Time: 25 minutes, plus 1 hour baking time
Makes: About 4 dozen cookies

Ingredients

2 1/2 cups all-purpose flour

1 teaspoon baking soda

1 teaspoon fine salt

2 sticks (8 ounces) unsalted non-hydrogenated margarine, at room temperature

1 1/4 cups granulated sugar

1 tablespoon light (or mild) molasses

2 teaspoons vanilla extract

1 1/2 cups vegan semisweet chocolate chips (about 10 ounces)

Directions

1. Heat the oven to 350°F and arrange a rack in the middle.

2. Place the flour, baking soda, and salt in a medium bowl and whisk to aerate and combine; set aside.

3. Place the margarine and sugar in the bowl of a stand mixer fitted with a paddle attachment and beat on medium-high speed until light and fluffy, about 3 minutes. Scrape down the sides of the bowl. Add the molasses and vanilla and beat on medium-high speed until combined, about 2 minutes, stopping to scrape down the sides of the bowl. Add the flour mixture and beat on low speed until just combined (do not overmix). Add the chocolate chips and mix on low speed until just combined.

4. Drop the crumbly dough 1 heaping tablespoon at a time onto an ungreased baking sheet, making sure the dough balls are spaced 2 inches apart. Roll each ball and press down to slightly flatten. Bake one sheet at a time until the cookies are just golden brown around the edges, about 11 minutes. Remove from the oven and let cool on the baking sheet for 5 minutes; transfer to a wire rack to cool completely. Repeat with the remaining dough, using a cooled baking sheet for each batch.

Rolling In Cookie Dough

Makes 1 cup packed cookie dough

Ingredients

1/2 cup unsalted cashews

1/4 cup rolled oats
1/4 cup spelt flour
1/2 tsp kosher salt
1 1/2 tbsp natural cane sugar
1/2 tsp pure vanilla extract
2 tbsp plus 1/2 tsp pure maple syrup
1/4 chocolate or dark chocolate chips

Directions

1. In a food processor add the cashews & oats until fine crumbs start to form

2. Add the salt, sugar & flour. process until just combined

3. Add the maple syrup & vanilla, process until combined

4. Add chocolate chips; either stir by hand or whirl in the processor

5. Form into mini cookie dough balls and store in the freezer

6. Chocolate chip cookie dough "blizzard" makes 2 servings

7. 3 peeled & frozen bananas cut into 1 inch chunks

8. 2 tbsp of almond milk or any non-dairy milk (more if needed)

9.2 tbsp cookie dough (from above recipe)

Assembly

1. In a food processor (a blender or immersion blender would probably work), add your 3 chopped frozen bananas. Process until blended, stopping to scrape down sides

2. While processing add milk until desired consistency is reached

3. Add in cookie dough and process until combined, you should have a soft serve consistency when done

4. Stir in as many cookie balls as you'd like & enjoy!

Cinnamon Rolls To Make Your Eyes Glaze

Makes: 18 rolls

Ingredients

3 1/4 cups all-purpose flour

1 package active dry yeast
1 cup almond milk
1/3 cup vegan butter
1/3 cup sugar
1/2 teaspoon salt
1/2 cup plain soy yogurt
2 tbsp butter, softened
3/4 cup packed brown sugar
1/2 tsp allspice
2 tsp ground cinnamon
1/4 tsp freshly grated nutmeg
1/2 cup chocolate chips or chunks
1/2 cup walnuts
4 tsp non-dairy cream
for the glaze
1 cup powdered sugar
2 tbsp almond milk
1 tbsp grand marnier

Directions

1. Combine 1-1/2 cups of the flour and yeast; set aside. In a saucepan heat milk, 1/3 cup butter, sugar, and salt until warm

(120 F. to 130 degrees F) and butter is almost melted. Add to flour mixture along with soy yogurt. Beat with an electric mixer on low speed 30 seconds, scraping bowl. Beat on high speed 3 minutes. Stir in as much of the remaining flour as you can

2. Turn dough out onto a lightly floured surface. Knead in enough remaining flour to make a moderately soft dough that is smooth and elastic (3 to 5 minutes total). Shape dough into a ball. Place dough in a lightly greased bowl; turn once. Cover and let rise in a warm place until double (1 to 1-1/2 hours)

3. Punch dough down. Turn out onto a lightly floured surface. Cover; let rest 10 minutes. Grease a 13x9x2-inch baking pan or (2) 8 inch rounds cake pans; set aside. Roll dough into 18x10-inch rectangle. Spread with softened butter. Combine brown sugar and spices; sprinkle onto dough. Sprinkle with chocolate and nuts (inside or they can be sprinkled on top once cut and placed into the pans). Tightly roll up into a spiral, starting from a long side. Pinch seams to seal.

4. Cut dough crosswise into 18 even slices - you can slice into 12 pieces for larger portions. Arrange slices, cut sides down, in the prepared baking pan. Cover and let rise until nearly double (about 30 to 40 minutes)

5. Brush rolls with half-and-half or light cream. Bake in a 350 degree F oven for 25 to 30 minutes or until golden. Invert rolls onto a wire rack or serving platter. Cool slightly in a medium bowl combine powdered sugar, almond milk and grand marnier - whisk until smooth, adding additional powdered sugar if needed to reach desired consistency - drizzle onto rolls

Tips

1. Up to 24 hours ahead, make and shape rolls.
2. Cover with oiled waxed paper; then with plastic wrap.
3. Chill in the refrigerator for 2 to 24 hours. Before baking, let stand for 20 minutes at room temperature.
4. Uncover and puncture any surface bubbles with a greased wooden toothpick.

Mini Nutmeg Donuts

Makes: 20 Donuts

Dry Ingredients:

1 Cup All Purpose Flour
1/2 Cup Sugar
1 1/2 tsp Baking Powder
1/4 tsp Salt
1/4 tsp (scant) Nutmeg
1 tiny pinch or shake Cinnamon

Wet Ingredients:

1/2 Cup Soymilk
1/2 tsp Apple Cider Vinegar
1/2 tsp Pure Vanilla Extract
Egg Replacer for 1 Egg
4 Tbs Earth Balance

Directions

1. Preheat oven to 350º F

2. In a large bowl, combine dry ingredients with a whisk to mix thoroughly. Combine wet ingredients in a small sauce pan over medium low heat and mix until earth balance is melted. This mixture should NOT get too hot, you should be able to stick your finger in the mixture. It should feel slightly warm.

3. Add wet to dry and mix until just combined. It should form a very soft dough. Using a tablespoon measure, scoop out dough into your ungreased nonstick mini-donut pan. Smooth out the

top of the dough with your fingers, this will make for more even, prettier donuts, but isn't crucial.

4.As you can see, the dough sits just below the rim. If you over fill, your donuts will come out looking like it has a little muffin top. Not the end of the world, but not very donut-like either.

5.Bake for 12 minutes. They should not be browned on top, but a tester will come out clean. Invert hot pan over a cutting board or cooling rack to release donuts. Allow to cool completely before decorating.

6.Time for toppings!

Glaze with Sprinkles

1/2 Cup Powdered Sugar
1 Tbs Soymilk
Bowl full of sprinkles (1/4 to 1/2 cup)

Whisk soymilk and powdered sugar together. Dip the "bottom" half of the donut into the glaze, let some drip off, then dip glaze-side down into sprinkles. Transfer to a wire rack that has been set on top of some parchment paper. The excess glaze will drip through the rack onto the paper for easy cleaning later.

No Kidding! Breakfast Pudding!

Serves: 2-4

Ingredients

19 ounces silken tofu
2 Tbsp raw cacao powder
3-4 Tbsp agave syrup
1-2 Tbsp light coconut milk
1/4 tsp pink salt
Fresh fruit: Add fresh organic raspberries and one sliced banana.

Directions

1. Add all the ingredients to your blender.
2. Blend and serve! You can also make this ahead of time and chill in fridge until ready to serve.

Options

* Blend in peanut or almond butter for a nutty accent.
* Add a dash of cinnamon for a spiced choco flavor.
* Add in raw coconut flakes for extra coconut-y flavor.
* Blend in a whole raw banana for a creamy sweet tropical accent.
* Blend in some raspberries for a softer berry-rific pudding.
* Blend in frozen fruit - like frozen bananas - for a soft serve shake-like parfait.

Nothin' Better Than Brownies

Total Time: 1 hour 30 minutes
Makes: 16 brownies

Ingredients

1 cup all-purpose flour

3/4 cup granulated sugar

1/2 cup natural unsweetened cocoa powder

1 teaspoon baking powder

1/4 teaspoon fine salt

1/2 cup unsweetened applesauce

1/4 cup maple syrup

1/4 cup plain, unsweetened soy or nondairy milk

1/4 cup vegetable oil, plus more for coating the pan

1 teaspoon vanilla extract

1/2 cup vegan semisweet chocolate chips

Instructions

1. Heat the oven to 350°F and arrange a rack in the middle. Coat an 8-by-8-inch square baking dish with vegetable oil; set aside.

2. Place the flour, sugar, cocoa powder, baking powder, and salt in a medium bowl and whisk to aerate and combine.

3. Place the applesauce, maple syrup, soy or nondairy milk, measured oil, and vanilla in a large bowl and whisk to combine. Add the flour mixture and fold with a rubber spatula until just combined (do not overmix). Fold in the chocolate chips. Scrape

the batter into the prepared baking dish and smooth out the top.

4.Bake in the oven until a knife inserted into the center comes out clean, about 35 minutes. Place the pan on a wire rack to cool for at least 30 minutes before serving. If not serving right away, cool completely, cover tightly, and store at room temperature. These brownies taste best if eaten within a day or two.

Captivating Cupcakes

Makes: 12

Ingredients

For the cupcakes

1/2 cup soy yogurt

2/3 cup almond milk

1/4 applesauce

3 tbsp canola oil

1/4 cup bourbon

1 tbsp vanilla

3/4 cup packed brown sugar

1/4 tsp all spice

1 1/4 cups flour

2 tbsp cornstarch

3/4 tsp baking powder

1/2 tsp baking soda

1/4 tsp salt

For the frosting

2 tbsp softened vegan butter

2 cups powdered sugar

3 tbsp almond milk

2 tbsp brown sugar

Toppings

1/4 cup pecans

1 tbsp brown sugar

Directions

1. Pre heat the oven to 350

2. Line a 12 cup muffin tin with liners

3. In a large bowl whisk together the yogurt, almond milk, applesauce, canola oil, bourbon, sugar & vanilla. sift in flour, cornstarch, baking powder, baking soda, all spice and salt. mix.

4. Fill cupcake liners 3/4 of the way full. bake 22-24 minutes or until a tooth pick comes out clean when tested in the center of the cupcake. transfer to a wire cooling rack and cool completely prior to frosting

To make the frosting

1. In the bowl of a mixer beat butter and powdered sugar for about 30 seconds

2. On low/medium speed beat in almond milk until the frosting comes together

3. Stir in brown sugar

4. Frost fully cooled cupcakes and top with brown sugar & pecans

Part 2

Introduction

Veganism is a practice followed by vegans who refrain from the intake of animal products. They can be classified into different categories, namely; dietary vegans, also known as strict vegetarians, are those who do not consume animal products and dairy products, ovo-lacto vegetarians are the ones who ingest dairy and egg products but do not consume any kind of animal products and lastly ethical vegans who also follow vegan diet and do not use animal products for any purpose like for food, entertainment or clothing.

In 1994, Donald Watson invented the name "Veganism" with the foundation of Vegan British society in England. Originally it meant "non-diary vegetarian" but then it referred, man should live without taking use of animals. The difference between vegans and vegetarian diet is that vegans exclude dairy and eggs products. Vegan diet is based on grains, beans, fruits and nuts. Meat analogues are formed from soya beans or wheat which are a common source of plant protein. Soya beans are a complete protein and contain all the amino acids that are needed by human beings thus can be relied for protein intake. They come in a variety of textures calculating upon the water content, from firm for stir-fries, to soft for garnishing the meals and desserts.

Vegan (egg-free) mayonnaise brands include, Nayonaise, Vegenaise, Miso Mayo and Plamil's Egg-Free Mayo. When the protein in eggs is heated it gets thickened and binds up with the other ingredients properly. Now for vegans, each egg in a recipe is replaced with a tablespoon of flaxseed meal mixed with three tablespoons of water.

Vegan Cheese

Vegan cheese is a cheese which does not have milk and animal based enzyme in it. To make it, animal genome is searched for milk protein DNA, and then sequences are chosen to synthesize the genes which are then inserted in yeast temporarily and produced using cellular machinery of baker's yeast.

This cheese is made from soya protein, and also from rice, almonds, nutritional yeast and other ingredients which are non dairy. Different types of vegan cheese are available from hard or firm which can be easily sliced to soft that can be used in lasagna. Even mozzarella is a type of it which can be used as a pizza topping. Vegan Cheese is becoming in demand.

Environment

Yeast will be grown in bioreactors not in an open environment. Thus it'll control the waste from the process more precisely. Moreover, Yeast's strains will be restructured from growing outside of the bioreactors. This process will be environment friendly thus will not be a contributor in global warming.

Cheese Addiction and Switching To Vegan Diet

Cheese is comprised of casein, it is an animal protein used in dairy products. During digestion, Casein is broken down into casomorphins that are protein fragments which have an opioid effect. It absorbs 10lb of milk to produce 1lb of cheese. During this process, water is evaporated and casein and fats are left concentrated. Thus dairy products have Opioids in huge amount. Opioids are also known as drugs that diminish the pain and lessen the signals going to the brain. It also functions as a histamine releaser which is why many people are sensitive to dairy substance. Cheese being addictive can also cause different types of cancers as it is claimed by scientific and nutritional research. Don't let dairy products control you, you can control them by little error and self discipline realizing that you are doing well for yourself, for animals, and for earth.

Thus many people are in their struggle to switch to a vegan diet. These are some tips that will help ease their battle:

- Start taking cooking classes, or find vegan cookbooks from book store or download them online and enjoy new and special recipes.
- Many alternative cheese options (mentioned further in this book) are healthy vegan cheese options and low in fat. You can easily get them from grocery stores.
- Enlighten yourself about your choice by reading and watching Vegan documentaries, such as Forks Over Knives or Earthlings.
- Wide open your eyes to new fruits and vegetables you haven't tried it yet!
- Get guidance from those who are already vegans by finding them in different social networks example face book, or set a meeting somewhere.
- Search for healthy plant based foods that you will love.

If you are deciding to follow vegan diet, implement all the rules that you will follow while having a balanced healthy diet for example lots of fruits, vegetables, whole grains, nuts, pulses, seeds, and cut off sweet and greasy foods to make sure that you are consuming all the nutrients that vegan diet is lacking in.

Why Vegan Cheese is the Healthier Option?

Plant fats are cholesterol free and very healthy, it functions to flow liquid inside your body with consistency. Whereas Animal fats have cholesterol that thickens the arteries and they aren't healthy comparatively. Animal proteins have less fiber and vitamins in contrast to Plant foods which have both of them considerable amounts. Plant Cheese will not cause constipation while animal protein can and cause colon cancer.

Vegan diets are likely to be higher in magnesium, vitamin C and E, dietary fiber, iron, phytochemicals, folic acid, and lower in long-chain omega-3 fatty acids, Vitamin D, zinc, calcium, calories, saturated fat, and vitamin B12. A smart and well organized vegan diet can even lessen the risk of heart diseases and is considered important for life cycle stages according to the American Dietetic Association, the Australian National Health and Medical Research Council, and Dietitians of Canada. It is stated by researches that vegans should take supplements in their diet or have B-12 fortified foods so that they get all nutrients that are inadequate in vegan's body.

Breakfast

Cheesy Tomato Stuffed Waffles

- 2 thin sliced tomatoes
- 4-6 slices vegan cheese (Daiya plain)
- 2 tablespoon coconut oil
- 1 teaspoon xanthan gum
- Salt to taste
- 3/4 cup club soda
- 1/3 cup coconut milk
- 2 cups all purpose, free of gluten flour
- 1 ½ teaspoons baking powder

Assembly

1. Sift together baking powder, flour, xanthan gum and salt.
2. Add milk, soda and oil and stir until just combined.
3. Transfer a small quantity (1/3 to 1/4 cup, according to the size of the waffle maker) into the waffle maker prepared beforehand.
4. Top with cheese slices and tomato, coat with another 1/4 cup of the mix.
5. Close and cook as per the maker instructions. Cooking each side for a couple of minutes should be sufficient.

Spicy Italian Sausage Patty With Mexican Cheese Dip

For the cheese dip

- 1 medium eggplant cut into 4 rounds, around 1/4-inch thick (half of the eggplant)
- Olive oil
- Sea salt
- 1.5 cups unsweetened almond or rice milk
- 2 Tbsp nutritional yeast (see instructions)
- 1/6 tsp fresh garlic power (I used crushed garlic from Whole Foods)
- 1/2 tsp cumin
- 1/2 tsp chili powder
- cornstarch (optional)
- 1/8 cup medium salsa

Method

1. Cut the eggplant into thin round skuces just under 1/4", then sprinkle both sides with a pinch of salt and place in a food strainer to draw out some of the left over moisture.
2. Let set for 8-13 minutes, then rinse with water and pat dry between two towels.
3. Preheat oven to broil and arrange the eggplant rounds on a baking with a little olive oil on both sides of the eggplant. Finally add a small amount of salt.
4. Broil on high for 4-5 minutes on each side, just as the rounds appear to have a golden brown tender texture, remove from the oven and wrap lightly in foil to steam.
5. After a few minutes, its time to peel the eggplant skin away. It should easily come off.

6. Place eggplant in a blender with the 1.5 cups almond milk, 2 Tbsp nutritional yeast, minced garlic, cumin and cornstarch and blend until smooth and creamy
7. Take sauce out of blender and place to a pan and warm over medium heat until slightly thickened and bubbly – about 5 minutes.
8. NOTE: you can add extra thickness by adding an additional 1 tsp cornstarch to a small bowl with a splash of almond milk and 2-3 Tbsp of the cheese mixture. Whisk and then stir back into the pot.
9. Once cooked and thickened, remove from heat and stir in DRAINED salsa (around ¾ of a small jar). Pour into a serving dish and top with a little hot sauce to complete the flavor.

Spice Mix

- 1 ½ tsp. garlic powder
- 1 ½ tsp. fennel, crushed
- ½ tsp. black pepper
- 1 tsp. salt
- 1 ½ tsp. sweet paprika
- 1 ½ tsp. smoked paprika
- ½ tsp. red pepper flakes
- 1 tsp. oregano
- 1/8 tsp. allspice

Sausage

- 2 tsp. + 2 tsp. olive oil
- 1 cup chopped mushrooms
- ¼ cup finely chopped onion
- 1 minced garlic clove
- 2 cups cooked or 1-15 oz. can of drained and rinsed black-eyed peas

- 1 Tablespoon paste of sun-dried tomato
- ¼ cup nutritional yeast
- ½ cup brown rice flour
- 1 tsp. xanthan gum
- 3 Tablespoon of vegan Worcestershire Sauce

Assembly

1. Mix all the ingredients of the spice mix and keep it aside.
2. Sauté the mushrooms onions and garlic with 2 teaspoon of olive oil, in a heated skillet until soft. Keep aside and cool it.
3. With a potato masher or a fork, mash up the black-eyed peas in a large bowl, if you're using a food blender, do a coarse chop, not a puree. Now add the brown rice flour, nutritional yeast, spice mix and tomato paste. Combine well.
4. Spray the xanthan gum and mix in it well.
5. Incorporate the sautéed vegetable mixture and blend in dry ingredients, Worcestershire sauce into the bowl and mix it all up well.
6. Split the mixture into 4 parts and shape into a log. Envelop the logs separately in foil and steam them for 15-20 minutes. You can use a metal steamer that sits on top of a big pot of steaming water.
7. Remove from the steamer and let them cool. Place in the refrigerator for a couple of hours or overnight. This will aid in firming up even more.
8. When set to use, unwrap and cook them as you wish. Cooked them on a grill pan and season with sautéed bell peppers and onions and mustard.

Mediterranean Style Polenta Stack

- ½ cup Polenta
- ½ cup water/vegetable broth
- 3 tablespoon nutritional yeast
- 1 teaspoon garlic powder
- 1 teaspoon onion powder
- 2 teaspoons hummus
- Salt and pepper to taste

1. Mix up the ingredients in a bowl and leave it for 5-7 minutes. Transfer the mixture into a saucepan and cook it up till it comes to a roaring simmer on medium heat. Stir continuously until the mixture is thick (for about 5-7 minutes) and reaches a mashed potato like consistency and pulls off the vessel easily.
2. Immediately pour the mixture into non stick cake tins and level them out. Put them in the fridge to cool for 5 minutes or longer(depending on when it is to be served).

For the topping

- 2 roasted capsicums, marinated in vinegar, salt, sugar and spices
- ½ cup chopped Roma tomatoes
- ½ cup purple onion
- Fresh Cilantro/ Basil/ Thyme leaves
- Avocado mixture
- Balsamic vinegar/pesto/ chili sauce

For the Avocado mixture

1. Take a ripe avocado and scoop out the contents. Add the juice of one lemon, 2 teaspoons fresh garlic and salt to taste. Mash it up nicely till it forms a smooth paste.

Assembly

1. Take out the cooled polenta base from the cake tins, add the roasted red peppers, avocado mixture, chopped tomato, onion and top it with the herb of your choice. Pour Balsamic vinegar/ pesto /chili sauce over it and it's ready to be served.

Vegan Omelet

It's important to use a non-stick frying pan to make the omelet come out of the pan whole.

- 6 ounces (1/2 package) silken tofu
- 1 tablespoon soymilk
- 1 tablespoon nutritional yeast
- 1 tablespoon potato or cornstarch
- 1 teaspoon tahini (optional)
- 1/8 teaspoon onion powder
- 1/8 teaspoon turmeric
- 1/4-1/2 teaspoon salt, or to taste
- 1 pinch smoked paprika (optional)
- 1 pinch black salt, optional
- Omelet filling of your choice (onion, tomatoes, bell peppers etc.)

Assembly

1. Combine together all the ingredients until soft using a hand blender.
2. Lightly oil a skillet and heat until very hot. In a circular motion, pour the batter into the middle of the skillet, using a spatula to level out the top. Place the filling over the batter, and decrease the heat.
3. Cook with cover for about 3-5 minutes, checking regularly. It is done when the edges leave the pan and the center is fully cooked, the base will be golden brown. Loosen the omelet when it's ready using the spatula to slide under it from each direction, and then fold over. Leave it for a minute or so then plate it out.

Main Dishes

Vegetable & Cheesy Rice Bake

- 1 finely chopped onion
- 1 tablespoon olive oil
- 2 sliced courgettes (zucchini)
- 1 diced aubergine (eggplant)
- 16 oz fresh tomatoes, chopped (or a 15 oz can chopped tomatoes)
- 7oz risotto rice
- 5oz grated vegan cheddar cheese (Daiya plain)

Assembly

1. Fry onions for 10 minutes in oil until they become soft and lightly brown. Then put in the courgettes and aubergine and fry until golden brown.
2. Put in the tomatoes and some seasoning, then cover and cook in low flame for 30 minutes. Uncover for the final 15 minutes if you're using fresh tomatoes. Heat oven to 200°C or 180°C.
3. In the meantime, add the rice to large pot of salted boiling water and cook for 20 minutes, or until the rice grains are tender. Drain the water out and add in two-thirds of the cheese.
4. Place the tomato and courgette mixture in an ovenproof dish. Dish out the rice mix and level it out. Shower the rest of the cheese over the mixture. Cook in the oven for 30 minutes until it starts to bubble and turns golden-yellow.

Italian Wonder Pot

- vegetable broth (4 cups)
- 2 Tablespoon olive oil
- Fettuccine (12oz.)
- 8 oz. chopped frozen spinach
- 1 can (28 oz.) diced tomatoes
- 1 onion(medium)
- 4 garlic cloves
- ½ Tablespoon dried basil
- ½ Tbsp dried oregano
- ¼ tsp red pepper flakes
- freshly cracked pepper to taste
- 3 oz. vegan tofu feta cheese

Tofu Feta Cheese

- 9 ounces firm tofu (275 g)
- ¼ cup lemon juice (60 ml)
- ½ cup water (125 ml)
- ½ cup apple cider vinegar (125 ml)
- 1 tbsp oregano

1. Start the pressing proccess with the Tofu.
2. Take the tofu out and drain of all water.
3. Put a towel, on a flat surface, place the tofu on top cover with another towel, clean towel on top of the tofu.
4. Place a bowl or anything heavy, such as cans or whatever.
5. Let the tofu sit for at least 30 minutes.
6. Cut the tofu into medium sized cubes.

7. Mix the remaining ingredients in a bowl or a container (the lemon juice, water, apple cider vinegar and oregano), now add the tofu, cover well and refrigerate for at least 2 hours.
8. It will taste better 2 or 3 days later.

Assembly

1. Add the vegetable broth to a large container. To make stirring easier later, break the fettuccine in half and then put it in to the pot.
2. Also add the olive oil, canned tomatoes (undrained), onion (sliced thinly), frozen spinach, basil, red pepper, garlic (finely sliced), oregano, and some freshly cracked black pepper.
3. Make sure the ingredients are fully immersed in the liquid, place a lid on top of the pot, and increase the flame to high.
4. Heat the mixture until it is boiling vigorously over high heat. Remove the lid and reduce the flame to medium.
5. Boil the mix over medium heat, without the cover, for 10-15 minutes, or until most of the liquid has been absorbed and the pasta has cooked.
6. Keep stirring frequently to avoid pasta sticking to the pot. But don't stir it too much or the pasta will become squashy.
7. As soon as the pasta is ready, shred the feta cheese over it and serve.

Vegetable Lasagna Recipe

- 12 Lasagna noodles
- 8 ounces fresh, sliced mushrooms
- 1 ½ cups yellow and red, chopped bell pepper –about 1 large
- 2 ½ cups diced zucchini– about 1 medium
- One 10 ounce pack of frozen spinach chopped – thawed & drained (squeeze)
- 1 ½ cup shredded carrot (2 small)
- 3/4 cup chopped onion
- 3 teaspoon minced garlic (4 cloves)
- 2 teaspoon finely chopped fresh thyme
- 3-4 Tablespoons olive oil
- 5 cups of tomato sauce (homemade or readymade) about two 26 ounce jars
- 3 cups vegan ricotta cheese
- 4 cups shredded mozzarella cheese
- Fresh nutmeg
- ½ cup Vegan Parmesan cheese (Goveggie brand)– plus 3 Tablespoons for topping
- Salt and fresh ground pepper

Riccota Cheese

- 2 cups cashews, pre-soaked for around 1½ hour
- 2 cloves of garlic
- 3 tbsp of lemon juice
- ¼ cup vegan soy or almond milk
- 1 tbsp maple syrup
- 1 tbsp virgin olive oil
- ½ tbsp crushed basil leaves

- 1/4 cup chives
- 1 tsp ground pepper
- ½ tsp sea salt

1. Add the cashews, lemon juice, garlic, vegan milk, olive oil, maple syrup, crushed basil, and chives a food processor until finely smooth.
2. If ricotta is not smooth enough, add a bit more vegan milk. It can take a couple of minutes to process the cheese properly.
3. Finally add salt & pepper, to taste.

Mozzarella Cheese

- ¼ cup raw cashews
- 1cup hot water
- 1 teaspoon lemon juice
- 1 small garlic clove
- ¾ teaspoon salt
- 2 tablespoon tapioca flour
- 3teaspoon olive oil
- 1 tablespoon nutritional yeast

1. Put all the above ingredients in a blender and mix for about 2-3 minutes or until it forms a smooth paste.
2. Transfer the mixture in a saucepan and cook on medium heat, stirring constantly.
3. After a minute or two, it will start clumping, keep stirring till it becomes nice and thick and starts leaving the sides of the saucepan.
4. Remove it from the heat, cool it and it is ready to be used.

Method

1. Boil the lasagna noodles in a big vessel of water for 10 minutes, according to the Method: on the box or until al

dente. Strain them and lay aside on a parchment paper lightly greased.
2. Heat a large skillet (12 inches) beforehand over medium high heat. Add one tablespoon olive oil, onion, mushrooms and green peppers. Cook while stirring for a couple of minutes, sprinkle salt and freshly ground pepper. Cook for another 2 minutes or until vegetables become softer and begin to develop a brownish color.
3. Finally add in the zucchini and carrots, a little more salt and pepper. Stir for a few minutes more until zucchini is tender. Put in the thyme and garlic, mix for a minute. Remove from heat, transfer the mixture into a bowl and keep it aside.
4. Keep oven preheated to 350°F. Combine together the ricotta, ½ cup parmesan cheese, 2 cups mozzarella cheese as well as the squeezed and chopped spinach, several shredding of nutmeg, ¼ teaspoon salt and 1/8 teaspoon white/black pepper. Blend together thoroughly and set aside.
5. Grease a 9×13″ baking dish with butter or non-stick spray. Spread one quarter of the tomato sauce on the base. Position four lasagna noodles (overlapping) on top of the sauce. Add one third of the ricotta mixture in dollops and evenly spread it. Distribute uniformly 1/3 of the vegetable mixture and then pour ¼ of the sauce. Repeat the procedure to make another layer. Then sprinkle on top with the extra parmesan and mozzarella cheese.
6. Cut out a foil large enough to cover the casserole. Line the side of the foil facing downwards with butter or non-stick spray and then place over the lasagna. Place the dish on center shelf of oven.
7. Bake for about 45-60 minutes or until bubbling hot. Then take out from the oven. Carefully remove foil, replace the casserole in the oven and let it bake until the top layer of cheese turns brown. This may take another 15-20 minutes.

8. Carefully remove the casserole from the oven and let it cool down before serving. Hope you enjoy this recipe!

Cheesy Rice Casserole

For The Rice

- 5 oz pack of Rice (you can use any of your choice)
- ½ Cup Creamed Corn
- ½ Cup Mild Enchilada Sauce
- 1-2 Tablespoon Mild Green Chiles
- ¼ Cup grated Vegan Parmesan (Go-Veggie brand)

For The Mushrooms

- 2 Portobello, chopped and stems removed
- 1 teaspoon Oil of your choice
- ⅛ teaspoon Garlic Powder
- ¼ teaspoon Onion Powder
- ¼ teaspoon Chili Powder
- ¼ teaspoon Salt
- ⅛ teaspoon Pepper

Toppings

- Vegan Shredded Cheddar Cheese (Daiya plain)
- Frozen or Fresh Corn
- 1 diced Roma Tomato
- 1 sliced Green Onion
- Vegan Sour Cream
- Parsley/ Cilantro for garnish

Sour Cream

- 1 cup whole raw cashews
- ½ cup water
- 1/6 cup fresh lemon juice

- ¼ cup raw macadamia nuts
- 1 tablespoon nutritional yeast
- ¾ teaspoon sea salt
- ½ teaspoon white pepper

1. Put raw cashews in an enclosed glass container and soak in water for 6 hours, in the fridge.
2. Draw off the water and wash. Put it in the blender along with all other ingredients: macadamia nuts, nutritional yeast, water, lemon juice, salt and pepper.
3. Mix together until even, 3 minutes or so. The mixture will be thick and rich. Avoid addition of water.
4. The sour cream will solidify up over a couple of hours. Store in a sealed container for up to 3 days.

Assembly

1. Cook rice according to package directions.
2. Sauté the mushrooms in a saucepan with 1 teaspoon oil, blend in the seasonings and stir fry till the mushrooms are brown and tender. Set it aside.
3. Keep the oven ready at 375 °F.
4. Add the creamed corn, green chilies, the enchilada sauce, and vegan parmesan to the cooked rice.
5. Grease an oven safe casserole with oil and evenly spread the rice mixture evenly.
6. Now top it with the Sautéed mushroom mixture.
7. Then put in the fresh (or frozen) corn and sprinkle with vegan mexican shredded cheese.
8. Cook in the oven until bubbling.
9. Top with green onions and fresh tomatoes.
10. Garnish with parsley and serve with vegan sour cream.

Grilled Spicy Cheese Shashlik

- 6oz vegan cottage cheese cubes
- 6 baby corns-blanched and chopped
- 5 tablespoon tomato ketchup
- 1 tablespoon Tabasco sauce
- 1½ tablespoon corn flour
- 1 green capsicum
- 1 red capsicum
- 1 tablespoon chili powder
- 1 tablespoon pizza seasoning
- Coriander leaves
- Salt to taste

Cottage Cheese

- 1 (11 1/2 ounce) box firm silken tofu
- 2/3 cup vegan mayonnaise (Vegenaise brand)
- 2 teaspoons onion powder
- 1 teaspoon garlic powder
- 1 teaspoon salt
- 1 teaspoon nutritional yeast
- 1 teaspoon dried dill

1. Crumble silk tofu into a bowl. Massage with your hands until consitency resembles cottage cheese curds.
2. Mix in all other ingredients until it looks like cottage cheese, adding extra vegenaise or water if required.
3. Sprinkle fresh herbs or seasonings.

Assembly

1. In a bowl add tomato ketchup, Tabasco sauce, red chili powder, pizza seasoning, corn flour, coriander leaves. In case you can't find pizza seasoning, you can use mixed herbs and chili flakes.
2. Mix all the ingredients. Corn flour helps to bind ingredients so that it does not fall off while grilling.
3. Add cheese cubes and coat well with marinate. Add the other vegetables too taking care that the cheese cubes don't break. You can also use other vegetables like mushrooms, broccoli or baby potatoes.
4. Skew bell pepper, baby corn and cheese on shashlik sticks.
5. Place the skewers on a tray and put the tray in a preheated oven at 180°c
6. Turn them around in between and grill till you get nice and black edges.

Quesadilla- Spicy Tortillas Filled With Cheesy Vegetables

- 2 cups of mixed finely chopped vegetables (zucchini, green and red bell peppers, baby corn, spring onions)
- Black Pepper
- Mixed Herbs
- Salt to taste
- Fresh Parsley (finely chopped)
- Tortillas
- Red chili sauce
- Mozarella Vegan Cheese
- Olive Oil

Mozzarella Cheese

- ¼ cup raw cashews
- 1 cup hot water
- 1 teaspoon lemon juice
- 1 small garlic clove
- ¾ teaspoon salt
- 2 tablespoon tapioca flour
- 3 teaspoon olive oil
- 1 tablespoon nutritional yeast

1. Put all the above ingredients in a blender and mix for about 2-3 minutes or until it forms a smooth paste.
2. Transfer the mixture in a saucepan and cook on medium heat, stirring constantly.
3. After a minute or two, it will start clumping, keep stirring till it becomes nice and thick and starts leaving the sides of the saucepan.

4. Remove it from the heat, cool it and it is ready to be used.

Assembly

1. Put all the vegetables in a bowl and add the salt, black pepper and mixed herbs and mix well.
2. Take two uncooked tortillas, cut them into small round discs.
3. Spread chili sauce on one of them, cheese and mixed vegetables.
4. Add another layer of cheese, and place the other tortilla on top.
5. Press a little so that it sticks. The quesadilla is ready to roast.
6. Apply a little oil to a preheated pan.
7. Place the quesadilla on to it and apply olive oil on it too.
8. Turn over till cooked and press a little so that the tortillas stick to each other.
9. Cut the quesadillas into four and serve hot.

Baked Vegan Cheesy Crisps

Makes about 40 to 50 small crackers

- 1/2 cup almond flour/meal
- 1 1/2 tsp. nutritional yeast
- 1/4 tsp. salt
- 1/8 tsp garlic powder
- 1/8 tsp smoked paprika
- 1/8 tsp ground black pepper
- 1 tsp olive oil
- 1 tablespoon water (slightly less or more as needed)

Assembly

1. Keep the oven heated to 350°F and take out a big baking tray.
2. In a medium sized bowl, whip together the nutritional yeast, almond meal, smoked paprika, garlic powder, salt and black pepper.
3. Blend the ingredients to make dough with olive oil and about 1 tablespoon of water.
4. Cautiously roll the dough out among 2 big parchment paper sheets to about 12" diameter paper-thin circle.
5. Take away the upper parchment paper and use a cutter to cut the dough into 1½ to 2 " squares.
6. Now place the parchment on the baking sheet. Bake for about 10 to 12 minutes or until the crackers are crisp and light golden, turning the tray once in between.
7. Cool before serving.

8. These crisps can be kept for up to 2 weeks in an airtight container at room temperature.

Cheesy Broccoli Tots With Cheddar Onion Sauce

Makes 33 to 35 tots. Serves 8

- ¾ cup raw almonds
- ¾ cup breadcrumbs
- 4½ cups broccoli florets
- 1¼ cups shredded cheddar cheese (Daiya plain)
- ¼ cup chopped sun-dried tomatoes
- ¼ cup fresh basil, chopped
- 1 teaspoon garlic powder

Cheddar Onion Sauce

- 1 tablespoon olive oil
- 2 teaspoon all-purpose flour
- 1 cup (250ml) soy milk
- 1 cup (85g) shredded vegan cheddar cheese
- 1 teaspoon to ½ tablespoon onion powder (depending on how much onion flavor you want)
- ¼ teaspoon white pepper (or cayenne pepper)
- ¼ teaspoon salt

Assembly

1. Chop the almonds in a food processor until they turn into small pieces about the size of rice.
2. After that, toast the bread, tear into smaller pieces and chop up in the processor until they are as small as peas.

3. Next, chop the broccoli florets in a blender until they turn into small pieces.
4. In a large container or bowl, mix together all the ingredients for the tots.
5. Preheat oven to 350° F. The tots can be cooked in two ways. Either on a large rimmed baking sheet or in a 24-hole mini muffin tin. If cooking on the baking sheet first line it with parchment paper and if cooking in the muffin tray spray it with cooking spray. The muffin tin makes rounder tots, but when cooked on the baking tray the tots are browner.
6. Take one and a half to two tablespoons of the mixed ingredients and make them into round balls until all the mixture in the bowl has been used up for the tots. Place all the balls in the parchment paper or muffin tray and bake for 20 to 30 minutes or until the tops are browned.

While the tots are baking, let's make the cheese sauce.

1. In a saucepan, add olive oil and place it on medium-high heat, then add the all purpose flour, and mix it with the oil at once. When the flour starts to simmer, add the milk and let it bubble. Lower the heat, and blend in the vegan cheddar cheese. Take out from heat and mix in the white pepper, salt and onion powder. Enjoy the tots with the cheese sauce.

Cheesy Vegetable Burgers

- 2 tablespoon olive oil
- 2 sliced leeks,
- 200g sliced mushrooms,
- 2 large carrots, grated and peeled
- 1 tablespoon seasoning (Schwartz Moroccan recommended)
- 1 tablespoon soya sauce
- 300g drained and rinsed canned beans (you can also try kidney or pinto)
- 100g vegan cheddar cheese, grated coarsely (Daiya plain)
- 200g (about 4 slices) bran bread (torn into pieces)
- Burger buns
- Lettuce
- Tomatoes

Chop the vegetables finely and use them as the base for a pasta sauce. Add the carrots into the mashed potatoes and use this mix to top pies.

Assembly

1. Heat 1 tablespoon of oil in a shallow pan on medium heat. Empty the vegetables, seasoning and soya sauce. Then cook for 10 minutes, stirring it occasionally, until soft. Put the vegetables into a food processor with the bread, beans and cheese. Season and blend to form a thick paste.
2. With wet hands, mould the mixture into 8 burger patties. These can be stored in the refrigerator for 2 days or frozen for up to 2 months.
3. To cook, heat some oil in a frying pan and fry on each side for 2-3 minutes or until crispy.
4. Serve with salad, mayo, ketchup and toasted buns.

Cheesy Onion Grilled Sandwich

Makes 4 sandwiches

- 8 slices sandwich bread (Any that you prefer)
- Vegan butter for brushing
- For the filling:
- ½ cup grated vegan cheese (daiya)
- ½ cup finely chopped spring onion whites
- 1 teaspoon vegan butter
- 2 teaspoon finely chopped green chilies
- ½ cup finely chopped cabbage
- ½ cup grated carrots
- ½ cup finely chopped spring onion greens
- 2 teaspoon chili sauce
- 1 tablespoon tomato ketchup
- Salt to taste

Vegan Butter

- 1/3 cup soy milk or raw cashews
- 2/3 cup of water
- 1 tsp. raw apple cider vinegar
- 1/4 teaspoon. sea salt
- 2/3 cup raw coconut oil, room temperature
- 1 tablespoon + 1 teaspoon organic canola oil (or any oil of your choice)
- 1 heaping teaspoon raw sunflower lecithin (or soy lecithin)
- 1/4 + 1/8 teaspoon guar gum (or xanthan gum)

Assembly

Combine the cashews with water in a food processor, until a smooth puree or paste is formed. The consistency should be like cream. (It's recommended you soak the cashews for a few hours). Pour out the cashew paste into a bowl and add the salt and apple cider vinegar. Mix and keep it aside for about 10 minutes. Doing this will thicken the paste a bit.

If the coconut oil is not at room temperature, you can warm it until it's just melts and then leave it to cool to room temperature. Or you can just leave it out of the fridge until it is at room temperature.

Add the canola oil, the coconut oil, the sunflower lecithin, the cashew paste and the guar gum to the food processor. Blend for about 2 minutes until it is completely even and smooth. Transfer the mixture into a mold and chill in the freezer until it is solid, that'll be about an hour or so. You can small plastic box for a tub effect or you can make short sticks using an ice cube mold. When the butter solidifies carefully pop it out of the mold.

This recipe will make 3 short sticks of butter. Wrap each in plastic wrap and put them in the freezer where they'll last for about a year. When you need one, transfer it to the fridge in an airtight container. And that's all. Enjoy!

- Warm butter in a non stick pan; add the spring onion whites and green chilies and sauté on medium flame for 1-2 minutes.
- Then add the cabbage, carrots, spring onion greens, mix up well and sauté for one more minute. While stirring, add the chili sauce, tomato ketchup, salt to taste and mix well on low flame for a minute.
- Now add the cheese to the mix, turn off the flame till the cheese melts. Let it cool and keep it aside. Split the filling into 4 identical portions.
- Butter two wheat bread slices lightly. On each bread slice place one portion of the filling.

- Butter two more bread slices and place them on the filling so that the side that is buttered is on the filling.
- Brush some butter on top of the prepared sandwiches and place them in a greased griller for 5-7 minutes or until bread is brown and crisp.
- Serve hot with tomato or chili sauce.

Mozarella Bread Pizza

- 4 slices brown bread (or sandwich bread)
- 1 cup grated vegan mozzarella cheese
- ½ cup chopped capsicum
- ½ cup sweet corn
- ½ cup olives
- ½ cup pizza sauce
- 2 tablespoon oil/butter
- ½ teaspoon oregano
- ½ teaspoons freshly ground black pepper
- ½ teaspoon all spice mix

Mozzarella Cheese

- ¼ cup raw cashews
- 1 cup hot water
- 1 teaspoon lemon juice
- 1 small garlic clove
- ¾ teaspoon salt
- 2 tablespoon tapioca flour
- 3 teaspoon olive oil
- 1 tablespoon nutritional yeast

1. Put all the above ingredients in a blender and mix for about 2-3 minutes or until it forms a smooth paste. Transfer the mixture in a saucepan and cook on medium heat, stirring constantly.
2. After a minute or two, it will start clumping, keep stirring till it becomes nice and thick and starts leaving the sides of the saucepan. Remove it from the heat, cool it and it is ready to be used.

Vegan Butter

- 1/3 cup soy milk or raw cashews
- 2/3 cup of water
- 1 tsp. raw apple cider vinegar
- 1/4 teaspoon. sea salt
- 2/3 cup raw coconut oil, room temperature
- 1 tablespoon + 1 teaspoon organic canola oil (or any oil of your choice)
- 1 heaping teaspoon raw sunflower lecithin (or soy lecithin)
- 1/4 + 1/8 teaspoon guar gum (or xanthan gum)

1. Combine the cashews with water in a food processor, until a smooth puree or paste is formed. The consistency should be like cream. (It's recommended you soak the cashews for a few hours). Pour out the cashew paste into a bowl and add the salt and apple cider vinegar. Mix and keep it aside for about 10 minutes. Doing this will thicken the paste a bit.
2. If the coconut oil is not at room temperature, you can warm it until it's just melts and then leave it to cool to room temperature. Or you can just leave it out of the fridge until it is at room temperature.
3. Add the canola oil, the coconut oil, the sunflower lecithin, the cashew paste and the guar gum to the food processor. Blend for about 2 minutes until it is completely even and smooth. Transfer the mixture into a mold and chill in the freezer until it is solid, that'll be about an hour or so. You can small plastic box for a tub effect or you can make short sticks using an ice cube mold. When the butter solidifies carefully pop it out of the mold.
4. This recipe will make 3 short sticks of butter. Wrap each in plastic wrap and put them in the freezer where they'll last for about a year. When you need one, transfer it to the fridge in an airtight container.

Assembly

1. In a heated frying pan, add half teaspoon of butter. To the melted butter, add the sweet corn, capsicum and olives, oregano, salt and pepper. Sauté for two minutes take it out in a bowl and keep aside. You can also use carrots, onions or mushrooms.
2. Toast the bread on a slightly buttered non stick pan until light brown. On the toasted bread, add pizza sauce, prepared vegetables and grated cheese.
3. Place the bread on the pan again on low flame and cover it for 2 minutes.
4. The cheese should be melted and it is now ready to be served.

Grape And Maple Syrup Cream Cheese Crostini

Ingredients

- 1 lb grapes
- 1 tablespoon fresh, chopped rosemary
- 2 tablespoon olive oil
- 1/2 teaspoon salt
- 8 oz vegan cream cheese (Daiya plain)
- 2 tablespoon maple syrup + more for drizzling
- 1/2 cup chopped and toasted hazelnuts
- thinly sliced, baguette

Assembly

1. Set oven to heat at 300° F.
2. Mix together rosemary, salt, grapes and olive oil.
3. Place the grapes on a baking tray and roast for 5-7 minutes.
4. Slightly toast the thinly sliced baguette in the preheated oven. You can apply oil or butter to the slices.
5. Blend together maple syrup, cream cheese and salt (if needed).
6. Spread honey and cream cheese on toasted baguette slices. Finally place the roasted grapes and toasted hazelnuts on top.
7. Trickle with maple syrup.

Southwestern Grilled Vegan Cheese Sandwich

Ingredients

- 1 small thinly sliced sweet potato,
- 1/2 cup sliced sweet bell peppers,
- 1 cup beans (kidney beans or black beans)
- 1/2 cup salsa
- 4 slices bread
- 1 – 2 tablespoons vegan margarine
- Vegan sliced cheese (Daiya)

Assembly

1. Spray a pan with vegetable oil and cook the sweet bell peppers and sweet potatoes until tender (5 – 10 minutes), keep the peppers and potatoes on a plate and set aside to cool.
2. In a bowl, blend the salsa and the beans and mash with a fork until smooth or a little course as you prefer.
3. Use the same pan, heat it up; Spread a blob of margarine on one side of each slice and place the two slices of bread with buttered side down, 1 or 2 thin slices of Daiya cheese, mashed beans and grilled sweet potatoes and again 1 or 2 thin slices of cheese. Cover with the second prepared bread, with the buttered side facing upwards.
4. Let the bread toast as you prefer. Keep checking to see when the side turns brown, the cheese should have also melted a little; turn the sandwich carefully and cook the other side too.

Dinner

Vegan Margherita Pizzas

Makes 4 individual pizzas.

Pizza Dough

- 2 Cups all purpose flour (organic)
- 1 Cup whole wheat flour (organic)
- 2 1/4 t. active dry yeast (1 packet)
- 1 cup lukewarm water
- 2 teaspoon sea salt
- 1 teaspoon agave\flaxseed
- 1 Tablespoon extra virgin olive oil (optional)

Mix all the ingredients and massage for 10 minutes. Cover it up and leave in a warm place for an hour to rise until the dough is double its volume. In the meantime let's see how to make the pizza sauce.

The Pizza Sauce

- one 14 ounce can tomatoes(crushed)
- 3 cloves garlic minced
- 1/2 teaspoon dried thyme
- 1/2 teaspoon dried oregano
- 1/2 teaspoon dried basil
- 1 teaspoon. extra virgin olive oil (optional)
- 1 teaspoon agave
- Salt and ground black pepper to taste
- 2 tablespoons of Mozzarella cheese

Mozzarella Cheese

- ¼ cup raw cashews
- 1 cup hot water
- 1 teaspoon lemon juice
- 1 small garlic clove
- ¾ teaspoon salt
- 2 tablespoon tapioca flour
- 3 teaspoon olive oil
- 1 tablespoon nutritional yeast

1. Put all the above ingredients in a blender and mix for about 2-3 minutes or until it forms a smooth paste. Transfer the mixture in a saucepan and cook on medium heat, stirring constantly.
2. After a minute or two, it will start clumping, keep stirring till it becomes nice and thick and starts leaving the sides of the saucepan. Remove it from the heat, cool it and it is ready to be used.

Method

1. In a small sauce pan sauté the garlic in a little olive oil on medium heat for a minute or two. Add all the herb seasonings, agave, salt and freshly grounded pepper.

Assembly

1. Preheat oven to 500°F.
2. After about an hour the dough should have doubled and is now ready to be rolled out. Knock it down (to remove air bubbles) and separate it into four equal portions. Place each portion on a floured surface and roll out the dough keeping the thickness as desired.
3. Add 1/4 of the pizza sauce on each of the pizza dough, fresh tomato slices, both tablespoons of the fresh mozzarella cheese and top it with fresh basil/oregano leaves.

4. Cook the pizzas in the oven on a baking tray for around 10-15 minutes or until the cheese turns brown and the crust is crispy.
5. Note: Be careful the pizzas are evenly browned and not burnt.
6. Remove pizzas from oven, sprinkle it with basil and serve hot!

Vegan Stuffed Shells

Serves 4

For the Filling

- Vegan Ricotta cheese
- cups cashews (soak overnight & drain)
- 2 cloves garlic
- 2 tablespoons lemon juice
- 2 tablespoons lemon
- ¼ cup water
- ½ cup firm tofu (crumbled)
- 1 teaspoon dried oregano
- ½ teaspoon red pepper flakes
- 1 cup raw, finely chopped kale (or spinach)
- handful of chopped chives and/or Basil
- salt & pepper, to taste

Ricotta Cheese

- 2 cups cashews, pre-soaked for around 1½ hour
- 2 cloves of garlic
- 3 tbsp of lemon juice
- ¼ cup vegan soy or almond milk
- 1 tbsp maple syrup
- 1 tbsp virgin olive oil
- ½ tbsp crushed basil leaves
- 1/4 cup chives
- 1 tsp ground pepper
- ½ tsp sea salt

1. Add the cashews, lemon juice, garlic, vegan milk, olive oil, maple syrup, crushed basil, and chives a food processor until finely smooth.
2. If ricotta is not smooth enough, add a bit more vegan milk. It can take a couple of minutes to process the cheese properly.
3. Finally add salt & pepper, to taste.

For the shells

- 16 jumbo shells
- a few cups of marinara sauce
- sprinkle of olive oil
- top with Goveggie! grated vegan parmesan cheese (optional)

Assembly

1. Preheat oven to 350°F.
2. Puree together the cashew s, vinegar, garlic and lemon juice in a blender or food processor, adding only little water. Add salt & pepper to taste.
3. Scoop out the cashew cream into a medium sized bowl and add in kale, red pepper flakes, oregano, chives, the crumbled tofu, and another few pinches of salt & pepper to taste. Mix well.
4. Cook the shells in salty water until al dente.
5. Prepare a baking bowl with a handsome amount of marinara sauce at the bottom.
6. Fill into each shell a few tablespoons of the mixture and put them into the baking bowl. Top each with a spoonful of marinara sauce and a drizzle with olive oil. Then cook in the oven for about 25 minutes.
7. Serve hot and enjoy.

Classic Baked Macaroni And Cheese

- 1 tablespoon olive oil
- 2 tablespoon all-purpose flour
- 1 tablespoon onion powder
- 2 teaspoon garlic powder
- 2 cups soy milk
- ½ cup shredded Vegan Cheddar cheese (Daiya)
- 2 Tbs. grated Parmesan cheese (Goveggie! brand)
- 2 cups elbow macaroni, cooked according to the Method: on the package
- ½ cup breadcrumbs

Assembly

1. Preheat oven to 350°F.
2. Coat a 6-cup baking dish with cooking spray. Add to the olive oil, onion powder, flour, and garlic powder in a saucepan and cook for 1 minute, whisking continuously. Slowly add in the milk. Increase to medium to high flame until the sauce starts to boil, whisking continuously. Reduce the flame to medium-low, and let it cook for about 5 minutes, stirring from time to time.
3. Turn the stove off and stir in Cheddar and Parmesan. Season with salt and pepper, if desired. Stir in macaroni. Transfer to prepared baking dish, and top with breadcrumbs. Lightly spray breadcrumbs with cooking spray. Bake 30 minutes, or until top begins to brown.

Broccoli Shells N' Cheese

- pasta 8 oz
- 1 broccoli (large crown)
- ½ (medium)onion
- 3 Tablespoon vegan butter
- All-purpose flour-3 tbsp.
- cups soy milk
- 8 oz. (2 cups) shredded vegan cheddar cheese (Daiya plain)
- Goveggie! vegan Parmesan cheese ¼ cup
- 1 teaspoon hot sauce (optional)
- salt and pepper according to taste

Vegan Butter

- 1/3 cup soy milk or raw cashews
- 2/3 cup of water
- 1 tsp. raw apple cider vinegar
- 1/4 teaspoon. sea salt
- 2/3 cup raw coconut oil, room temperature
- 1 tablespoon + 1 teaspoon organic canola oil (or any oil of your choice)
- 1 heaping teaspoon raw sunflower lecithin (or soy lecithin)
- 1/4 + 1/8 teaspoon guar gum (or xanthan gum)

1. Combine the cashews with water in a food processor, until a smooth puree or paste is formed. The consistency should be like cream. (It's recommended you soak the cashews for a few hours). Pour out the cashew paste into a bowl and add the salt and apple cider vinegar. Mix and keep it aside for about 10 minutes. Doing this will thicken the paste a bit.
2. If the coconut oil is not at room temperature, you can warm it until it's just melts and then leave it to cool to room

temperature. Or you can just leave it out of the fridge until it is at room temperature.

3. Add the canola oil, the coconut oil, the sunflower lecithin, the cashew paste and the guar gum to the food processor. Blend for about 2 minutes until it is completely even and smooth. Transfer the mixture into a mold and chill in the freezer until it is solid, that'll be about an hour or so. You can small plastic box for a tub effect or you can make short sticks using an ice cube mold. When the butter solidifies carefully pop it out of the mold.

4. This recipe will make 3 short sticks of butter. Wrap each in plastic wrap and put them in the freezer where they'll last for about a year. When you need one, transfer it to the fridge in an airtight container.

Assembly

1. Bring a big pot of salty water to boil. Wash the broccoli well and cut them into small florets.
2. To save time and dishes, cook the broccoli and pasta in the same pot. Put the pasta when the water is boiling vigorously. After 6-8 minutes, add the broccoli and keep for 2-3 minutes more. Pour the contents into a colander and keep aside.
3. For the cheese sauce, cook finely diced onions in butter until tender. Then add flour, stir continuously for 2 minutes till it forms a smooth paste taking care it does not scorch.
4. Blend in the milk and beat till all flour clumps dissolve. Simmer the mixture while adding fresh cracked black pepper.
5. As soon as the sauce thickens and coats the back of a spoon, add the cheese.
6. Add in the grated and shredded cheese and whip till it melts completely. Add salt and hot sauce for seasoning.
7. Finally put in the drained broccoli and pasta to the prepared cheese sauce.

Cream Cheese Mashed Potato

- 1 teaspoon olive oil
- 2 medium, chopped yellow onions
- 2½ lb. potatoes, peeled and cut into small cubes
- 1¼ lb. cauliflower, cut into small florets
- ¼ cup + 1 tablespoon almond milk
- 3 oz. Vegan Cream Cheese (Daiya Cream Cheese)
- 1 roasted chopped red pepper
- ½ teaspoon salt
- ½ teaspoon black pepper freshly ground

Assembly

1. In a large frying pan heat the olive oil over medium heat.
2. Fry the onions till golden brown, stirring in between.
3. In a saucepan, boil the potato cubes and cauliflower florets until soft (check by piercing it with a fork).
4. Strain the water from the vegetables then, again, place them in the saucepan over medium heat until dry.
5. Mash the potatoes using a potato masher to remove the large lumps along with the almond milk.
6. Incorporate the cream cheese to the potato mash and keep on mixing till the mixture is evenly spread.
7. Blend in the onions and chopped peppers; add salt and black pepper for seasoning into the mixture.

Desserts

Raw Vegan Cheesecake

For Cheesecake

- 2 ½ cups raw cashews or macadamia nuts
- 1 tablespoon vanilla bean paste
- 1/2 cup (pure) maple syrup or raw agave
- 1/4 cup + 1 tablespoon melted coconut oil
- 1/2 cup lemon juice
- 1/4 cup water
- 1/8 teaspoon salt
- Blended strawberries, sweetener (for sauce) [optional]

For Crust

- 1/2 cup pitted dates
- 1/2 cup almonds
- 1/16 teaspoon salt
- 1/4 teaspoon pure vanilla extract
- about 1 tablespoon water (if needed)

Assembly

For Graham Cracker Crust

1. Plaster a 9-inch (round) springform pan with parchment paper, and keep aside.
2. Blend all the crust ingredients (except water) in a high-quality mixer, until small pieces are formed. If the mix is too dry, then add the water.
3. Empty the crust mix into the ready pan and press.
4. Then cover up and freeze until needed.

For Cheesecake

1. In a bowl, keep the cashews completely submerged underwater for 8 hours or overnight.
2. Then drain the water and pat to dry completely.
3. Combine all ingredients in a high-quality blender and mix for about 6 to 7 minutes, stopping from time to time.
4. Pour the mix into the prepared graham cracker crust.

The raw cheesecake can be stored in the freezer for up to 2 weeks. Don't forget to thaw for 15 to 20 minutes before serving.

Chocolate-"Cheesecake" Bars With Pine Nuts

- 1 cup pastry flour (whole-wheat)
- 1 cup sugar
- 4 ounces of vegan cream cheese (Daiya)
- 1 tablespoon vanilla extract
- 1/2 teaspoon almond extract
- 2/3 cup silken soft tofu
- 1/2 teaspoon baking powder
- 2 tablespoon vegetable shortening non-hydrogenated
- 2 tablespoon canola oil
- 1/2 cup slightly toasted pine nuts
- 2 tablespoon bitter dark chocolate chopped (Trader Joe's variety)
- Salt(pinch)

Assembly

1. Blend together the shortening, sugar and oil in a bowl and beat until fluffy with a hand-mixer or electric-mixer at low setting.
2. Next put in the cream cheese and beat until evenly blended.
3. Incorporate the tofu in three portions, mixing well after every addition.
4. Add in the cocoa powder and the vanilla and almonds extracts, and mix up well.
5. In another container, combine the baking powder, flour, and salt.
6. Now put in flour in the cocoa cheese mixture, while gently stirring.

7. Add in the bitter chocolate and the pine nuts. (The bitter chocolate gives the brownies a nice chocolaty taste without making them too sweet).
8. Empty the batter into a 9-inch oiled, square baking pan, and level out the top with a spatula.
9. Bake in the oven preheated to 350°F for about half an hour or until the top feels stiff.
10. Remove and cool on a stand for about 15-20 minutes before cutting in.

Cherry Cheesecake Cookies

- ¾ cup+ 2 tablespoon All-Purpose Flour
- ½ teaspoon Baking Powder
- ¼ teaspoon Salt
- ½ package (4 oz.) Vegan Cream Cheese (Daiya plain)
- ½ cup + 1 tablespoon, Vegan Butter
- ⅓ cup+ 1 tablespoon Sugar
- ⅛ cup Silken Tofu, blended until smooth
- ½ teaspoon Vanilla Extract
- ¼ cup Graham Cracker Crumbs
- 1 20 oz. can of Cherry Pie filling, drained

Vegan Butter

- 1/3 cup soy milk or raw cashews
- 2/3 cup of water
- 1 tsp. raw apple cider vinegar
- 1/4 teaspoon. sea salt
- 2/3 cup raw coconut oil, room temperature
- 1 tablespoon + 1 teaspoon organic canola oil (or any oil of your choice)
- 1 heaping teaspoon raw sunflower lecithin (or soy lecithin)
- 1/4 + 1/8 teaspoon guar gum (or xanthan gum)

Combine the cashews with water in a food processor, until a smooth puree or paste is formed. The consistency should be like cream. (It's recommended you soak the cashews for a few hours). Pour out the cashew paste into a bowl and add the salt and apple cider vinegar. Mix and keep it aside for about 10 minutes. Doing this will thicken the paste a bit.

If the coconut oil is not at room temperature, you can warm it until it's just melts and then leave it to cool to room temperature. Or you can just leave it out of the fridge until it is at room temperature.

Add the canola oil, the coconut oil, the sunflower lecithin, the cashew paste and the guar gum to the food processor. Blend for about 2 minutes until it is completely even and smooth. Transfer the mixture into a mold and chill in the freezer until it is solid, that'll be about an hour or so. You can small plastic box for a tub effect or you can make short sticks using an ice cube mold. When the butter solidifies carefully pop it out of the mold.

This recipe will make 3 short sticks of butter. Wrap each in plastic wrap and put them in the freezer where they'll last for about a year. When you need one, transfer it to the fridge in an airtight container.

Assembly

1. Mix salt, flour and baking powder in a bowl. Then set it aside.
2. Whip cream cheese, sugar and butter in a bowl with the help of an electric mixer for two minutes on medium speed till it has a smooth and silky texture. Then mix in the vanilla and tofu till completely blended. Lower the speed while adding flour mixture and whisk until incorporated. Wrap half of the kneaded dough in a plastic sheet and chill until it becomes firm.
3. The oven should be preheated at 350°F
4. Add graham crackers to a blender until it gets powdered.
5. Make balls out of the other half of the dough with a 1½-2" scoop and roll into the graham cracker crumbs. Place the balls directly on the cookie sheet. The dough being really should be handled minimally.
6. Make a small well in each ball and set three cherries into it. Place the cookies a little apart (2 inches) from each other to allow for space while baking.

7. Bake for 12-15 minutes, rotating the tray for even baking. Let the cookies cool for sometime before making it uniform using a round biscuit cutter.
8. Make balls out of the other half of the dough with a 1½-2" scoop and roll into the graham cracker crumbs. Place the balls directly on the cookie sheet. The dough being really should be handled minimally.
9. Make a small well in each ball and set three cherries into it. Place the cookies a little apart (2inches) from each other to allow for space while baking.
10. Bake for 12-15 minutes, rotating the tray for even baking. Let the cookies cool for sometime before making it uniform using a round biscuit cutter.

Frosted Cream Cheese Butternut Cookies

Serves: 16 cookies and 2.5 extra cups of frosting

For the cream cheese frosting:

- 225 g vegan cream cheese (Daiya plain)
- ¾ cup vegan butter
- 1 teaspoon vanilla extract
- 2 tablespoon soya milk
- 2½ cups icing sugar

Vegan Butter

- 1/3 cup soy milk or raw cashews
- 2/3 cup of water
- 1 tsp. raw apple cider vinegar
- 1/4 teaspoon. sea salt
- 2/3 cup raw coconut oil, room temperature
- 1 tablespoon + 1 teaspoon organic canola oil (or any oil of your choice)
- 1 heaping teaspoon raw sunflower lecithin (or soy lecithin)
- 1/4 + 1/8 teaspoon guar gum (or xanthan gum)

Combine the cashews with water in a food processor, until a smooth puree or paste is formed. The consistency should be like cream. (It's recommended you soak the cashews for a few hours). Pour out the cashew paste into a bowl and add the salt and apple cider vinegar. Mix and keep it aside for about 10 minutes. Doing this will thicken the paste a bit.

If the coconut oil is not at room temperature, you can warm it until it's just melts and then leave it to cool to room temperature. Or you can just leave it out of the fridge until it is at room temperature.

Add the canola oil, the coconut oil, the sunflower lecithin, the cashew paste and the guar gum to the food processor. Blend for about 2 minutes until it is completely even and smooth. Transfer the mixture into a mold and chill in the freezer until it is solid, that'll be about an hour or so. You can small plastic box for a tub effect or you can make short sticks using an ice cube mold. When the butter solidifies carefully pop it out of the mold.

This recipe will make 3 short sticks of butter. Wrap each in plastic wrap and put them in the freezer where they'll last for about a year. When you need one, transfer it to the fridge in an airtight container.

For the cookies

- ½ cup vegetable oil
- 1 cup butternut squash purée
- ¾ cup sugar
- ½ teaspoon cinnamon
- ½ teaspoon ginger
- ¼ teaspoon cloves
- ¼ teaspoon nutmeg
- ¼ teaspoon allspice
- 1 teaspoon baking powder
- ½ teaspoon salt
- 2½ cups unbleached all purpose flour

To make the frosting:

- Whip the cream cheese in an electric mixer for a minute to break it up. Put in the vegan butter and whip until soft and fluffy.
- To this mixture add the soy milk, vanilla extract. Add icing sugar ½ cup at a time until the frosting is smooth and creamy.

- Then set it aside.

For the cookies:
- Keep oven ready at 350°F.
- Combine the sugar, butternut squash purée, and oil and mix evenly.
- Add in cloves, allspice, ginger, cinnamon and nutmeg and stir.
- Blend in salt, flour, and baking powder.
- Measure out 3 tablespoon sized lump to create the cookies. Level out the cookies so that they bake uniformly.
- Bake for about 15 minutes, and then let cool on a wire stand. Once cooled wholly, ice with vegan cream cheese frosting.

Creamy Vegan Garlic Pasta With Roasted Tomatoes

- 3 cups grape tomatoes, halved
- 10 ounces whole wheat pasta
- Olive oil
- 2 medium shallots, diced
- 8 large cloves garlic, minced/grated
- Sea salt and black pepper
- 3-4 Tbsp unbleached all purpose flour (or another thickener of choice)*
- cups unsweetened plain Almond Breeze (you could also sub up to 1 cup with veggie stock)

Assembly

1. Preheat oven to 400 degrees and In a bowl toss tomatoes in with a Teaspoon of olive oil and a pinch of salt. Place on a tray with no stick oil and bake for 20 minutes while you make the rest of the dish.
2. In a large pot of water, cook the pasta until reaching a boiling point. Once done, drain with a strainer, cover and set aside.
3. At the same time, prepare the sauce. In a large frying pan over medium heat, add 1 Tablespoon olive oil and the garlic plus shallot. Add in a small pinch of salt and mix constantly, cooking for 3-4 minutes until creamy and aromatic.
4. Mix in 3 Tbsp white flour and stir with a whisk. Once consistent, gently whisk in the almond milk pouring in drops so clumps don't form. Add another pinch of salt and some black pepper, lower to a warm simmer and cook for another 4-5 minutes.
5. To make the sauce extra creamy, transfer sauce to a blender or food proccesor to blend the sauce until thick and

consistent. Place back in a frying pan and put heat to a warm simmer until thickness is acheived. Taste and adjust seasonings as needed.
6. Finally add pasta and roasted tomatoes and mix in.
7. Serve and sprinkle with more black pepper, fresh basil and Goveggie! vegan parmesan cheese.

Creamy Butternut Squash Linguine

- 2 tablespoons olive oil
- 1 tablespoon finely chopped fresh sage
- 2 pound butternut or kabocha squash, peeled, seeded, and cut into small ½-inch pieces (about 3 cups)
- 1 medium yellow onion, chopped
- 2 garlic cloves, pressed or chopped
- ⅛ teaspoon red pepper flakes (up to ¼ teaspoon for spicier pasta sauce)
- Sea salt and/or kosher salt
- Freshly ground black pepper
- 2 cups vegetable broth
- 12 ounces whole grain linguine or fettucine
- Optional additional garnishes: shaved Parmesan or Pecorino and/or smoked salt

Assembly

1. Add both tablesppons of oil in a large frying pan over medium heat, add in the sage and spread around to coat. Let the sage cook well before moving it to a small bowl. Sprinkle in a pinch of sea salt and set aside.
2. Add squash, onion, garlic and chopped red pepper to a frying pan. Season with a pinch of sea salt. Cook while stirring lightly for about 7- 9 minutes. Add vegetable broth. Bring the pan to a boil, then lower heat until liquid is decreased by half, about 15 to 20 minutes.
3. At the sametime, bring a large pot of water to a boil and cook the pasta, add in some salt. Drain with a strainer, reserving 1 cup cooking liquid.
4. Once the squash blend is finished cooking, turn off the heat and let it cool lightly. Transfer the mixturre of the pan to a

blender or food proccesor. Reserve the frying pan. Blend the mix until consistent, finally season with a bit of salt and pepper to taste.

5. Add in pasta, squash blend and ¼ cup cooking liquid in the reserved pan and simmer over medium heat, Add more pasta and liquid if nedded, make sure sauce coats the pasta, about 2 minutes.
6. Fianlly add fried sage over pasta, serve with more black pepper and Goveggie! Parmesan or salt, if desired.

Creamy Avocado Pasta

- 9 ounces (255 g) uncooked pasta (use gluten-free, if desired) or 1-2 medium zucchini (if making zoodles, see tip)
- 1 to 2 cloves garlic, to taste
- 1/4 cup fresh basil leaves, plus more for serving
- 1-2 tablespoons fresh lemon juice, to taste
- 1 tablespoon extra-virgin olive oil, plus more if needed
- 1 ripe medium avocado, pitted
- 1/4 to 1/2 teaspoon (1 to 2 mL) fine-grain sea salt, to taste
- Lemon, for serving

Assembly

1. Boil a large pot of water, add some salt and cook the pasta on medium heat for around 5-8 minutes.
2. In the meantime, lets prepare the sauce: In a food processor or blender, combine the garlic and basil and blend until fairly minced.
3. Add the lemon juice, oil, avocado meat, and 1 tbsp water and pulse until consisent and smooth. If add a small bit more oil if needed. Season with sea salt to taste.
4. Drain the pasta with a strainer and return to it to the pot. Add the finished sauce and mix until well combined. If needed, lightly reheat the pasta if it is too cool.
5. Top with lemon juice, and fresh basil leaves, serve and enjoy!

Vegan Meatloaf

Cooking time: 50 minutes

Servings: 8

Ingredients:

For the meatloaf:

- 1 cup canned or cooked chickpeas, drained and rinsed
- 1 cup canned or cooked kidney beans, drained and rinsed
- 1 cup ground flaxseed
- 1 cup nutritional yeast
- 1/2 cup tahini
- 1/4 cup tamari or soy sauce
- 1/4 cup unsweetened plant milk of your choice
- 2 teaspoons onion powder
- 2 teaspoons garlic powder
- 1/4 teaspoon ground black pepper

For the glaze:

- 1/2 cup ketchup
- 2 tablespoons cane, coconut or brown sugar

- 1 teaspoon onion powder
- 1 teaspoon garlic powder
- 1/2 teaspoon paprika

Instructions:

1. Put chickpeas, beans into a mixing bowl and mash with a fork or a potato masher.
2. Add the rest of the meatloaf ingredients and mix until well combined (you can also blend all the ingredients in a food processor).
3. Press the mixture firmly in a lined 9×5-inch loaf pan (feel free to place the mixture onto a lined baking sheet and form it into a loaf pan with your hands).
4. In order to make the glaze just mix all the ingredients in a mixing bowl until well combined
5. Preheat the oven to 350F. Spread the glaze evenly over the top and bake for 50 minutes.
6. Once cooked, remove from the oven and allow vegan meatloaf to cool for at least 5 minutes before removing it from the loaf pan.

Nutritional info (per serving): 172 calories; 6 g fat; 21 g carbohydrate; 10 g protein

Baked Squash

Cooking time: 2 hours 30 minutes

Servings: 4

Ingredients:

- 1 butternut squash
- olive oil
- 1 red onion
- 1 clove garlic
- 1 bunch fresh sage
- 10 sun-dried tomatoes
- 2.65 oz packed chestnuts or pecans
- 2.65 oz basmati rice
- 2.65 oz dried cranberries
- 1 pinch ground allspice
- red wine

Instructions:

1. Wash the squash, carefully cut it in half lengthways, remove and reserve the seeds. Use a spoon to score and scoop some flesh out, making a gully for the stuffing all along the length of the squash.

2. Finely chop the scooped-out flesh, put into a frying pan and fry on a medium heat with 2 tablespoons of oil.
3. Peel, finely chop and add onion, garlic, and stir regularly while you pick sage leaves and finely chop them with the sun-dried tomatoes and chestnuts.
4. Put into the pan with rice, cranberries and allspice; add a good pinch of sea salt and black pepper and a swig of red wine, mix well. Fry for 10 minutes, stirring occasionally, or until softened.
5. Pack the mixture tightly into the gully in two squash halves, then press halves firmly back together.
6. Rub the squash skin with a little oil, salt, pepper, and if you've got them, pat on any extra herb leaves you have to hand.
7. Put squash into the centre of a double layer of tin foil, tightly wrap it up.
8. Preheat the oven to 350F and bake for around 2 hours, or until soft and cooked through.
9. Once ready, take squash to the table, carve into nice thick slices and serve with all the usual trimmings.

Nutritional info (per serving): 245 calories; 5.1 g fat; 46.2 g carbohydrate; 5.8 g protein

Caesar Salad

Cooking time: 2 hours 30 minutes

Servings: 4

Ingredients:

- 1 cup raw cashews
- 1 cup non-dairy milk
- 2 tablespoons lemon juice
- 3 cloves garlic
- 2 teaspoons Dijon mustard
- 5 kalamata olives
- salt & pepper to taste
- romaine lettuce
- 3 slices whole-grain bread
- handful croutons

Instructions:

1. Soak cashews for at least 4 hours (the longer you soak them, the easier it will be to blend into the final dressing). Once soaked, drain the soaking liquid.
2. Combine all ingredients (except lettuce and bread in a high-powered blender or a food processor, and blend for couple of minutes, until cashews to turn into a creamy sauce with no chunks remaining.

3. If the mixture is too thick, slowly add several tablespoons water at a time and continue blending until it has the perfect salad dressing consistency. Adjust the seasoning.
4. Cover and refrigerate (cashew sauces tend to get much better after chilling for several hours. It can be saved (sealed) for several days in the refrigerator).
5. When ready to serve, chop the romaine lettuce and put it into a large bowl with as much dressing as you'd like. Toss and evenly coat the lettuce.
6. Garnish with homemade whole wheat croutons (below).

Nutritional info (per serving): 543 calories; 29.9 g fat; 57.4 g carbohydrate; 23 g protein

Vegan Cobb Salad

Cooking time: 2 hours 30 minutes

Servings: 4

Ingredients:

- 6 cups chopped fresh spinach (or another salad green for the base)
- 1 cup mandarin oranges, drained
- 1/3 cup sliced black olives
- 1/2 cup chopped sweet onion, tossed in black pepper
- 1 avocado, chopped, tossed in the juice of 1 large lemon
- 1 cup cherry tomatoes, halved
- 3/4 cup tempeh bacon bits
- 1 cup chilled kidney beans, drained
- 1 cup palm hearts, diced, tossed in 1/8 teaspoon turmeric + 1 teaspoon olive oil + 1 tablespoon apple cider vinegar + 1 tablespoon nutritional yeast

Instructions:

1. Toss spinach in a light salad dressing (only if serving immediately).
2. Toss half palm heats in a yellow turmeric mix.

3. Continue assembling salad by adding all ingredients in thin rows across the top.
4. Once done, it is ready to serve.

Nutritional info (per serving): 268 calories; 19 g fat; 21 g carbohydrate; 8 g protein

Veggie Dogs

Cooking time: 30 minutes

Servings: 6

Ingredients:

- ½ medium onion, coarsely chopped
- 3 cloves garlic
- 3/4 cup cooked pinto beans, well-drained
- 1/2 cup plus 2 tablespoons water
- 2 tablespoons coconut aminos or soy sauce
- 1 tablespoon tomato paste
- 2 teaspoons smoked paprika
- 1 teaspoon ground coriander
- 1 teaspoon ground mustard
- 1/2 teaspoon white or black pepper
- 1/4 teaspoon celery seed
- 1/4 teaspoon mace
- 1/8 teaspoon hickory smoked salt (optional but good)
- 1 cup vital wheat gluten
- 1/3 cup oatmeal rolled or quick oats, uncooked
- 2 tablespoons nutritional yeast
- 1 tablespoon ground flax seeds

Instructions:

1. Put onion, garlic into a food processor and pulse to chop finely.
2. Heat a small non-stick skillet. Add onion, garlic and cook until onion is softened, for about 3 minutes. Transfer onion mixture back to a food processor.
3. Add pinto beans, water, coconut aminos or soy sauce, tomato paste, all seasonings to the food processor and blend until it's a thin paste.
4. Combine the remaining ingredients (gluten, oatmeal, yeast, and flax) in a large mixing bowl.
5. Add contents of the food processor and stir until combined (if it seems that there's not enough moisture, add another tablespoon or two of water).
6. Knead in a bowl for about 2 minutes until a heavy gluten dough is formed.
7. Put steamer into a pot of water and bring the water to a boil.
8. Cut off 8 pieces of aluminum foil or parchment paper, each about 6 inches long and divide the gluten into 8 equal pieces. Place a piece of foil or parchment on the counter.
9. Roll a piece of gluten between the palms of your hands until it's about the size and shape of a hot dog, and place it on the foil/paper and roll up.
10. Roll the tube back and forth, pressing lightly with your hands, to give it an even shape, and then twist the ends closed.
11. Repeat with the remaining gluten to form 8 veggie hot dogs.
12. Put all veggie dogs on the top of a steamer, cover, and steam for 45 minutes. Remove from heat and allow to cool slightly before unwrapping.
13. Store veggie dogs in a covered container in a refrigerator. Warm gently in a frying pan or a microwave or on a grill before serving.

Nutritional info (per serving): 136 calories; 1.5 g fat; 23.1 g carbohydrate; 8.4 g protein

Eggplant Parmesan With Cashew Ricotta

Cooking time: 1 hour 45 minutes

Servings: 4

Ingredients:

- 3 tablespoons olive oil
- 1/2 medium onion
- 2 garlic cloves, minced
- 1 (28 oz) can crushed or diced tomatoes
- 2 large eggplants
- salt
- fresh ground pepper
- 1 teaspoon dried oregano, or 1 tablespoon minced fresh oregano
- 2 tablespoons minced fresh flat-leaf parsley
- 1 bunch fresh basil, stemmed and leaves torn into large pieces
- 1 cashew ricotta
- 1 cup dried bread crumbs
- 1/2 cup non-flavored, non-dairy milk

For the cashew ricotta:
- 3/4 cup raw cashew pieces (4 oz)
- 2 tablespoons fresh lemon juice
- 1 garlic clove
- 1 tablespoon extra-virgin olive oil
- 8 oz extra-firm tofu, drained
- 1/2 teaspoon salt
- 2 grinds black pepper

Instructions:

To make the cashew ricotta:

1. In a food processor, combine cashews, 2 tablespoons lemon juice, 1 garlic clove, 1 tablespoon extra virgin olive oil, tofu, 1/2 teaspoon salt and 2 grinds of pepper.
2. Process until smooth and creamy, for 2-3 minutes. Set aside.

To make the eggplant:

3. In a large skillet, heat 1 tablespoon olive oil on a medium heat.
4. Add onion and saute until soft and translucent for about 4-5 minutes. Add garlic and saute for 1 minute.
5. Add tomatoes, their juices and cook, stirring occasionally until thick, for 25-30 minutes.
6. Let cool, then transfer to a blender or a food processor and blend until smooth.
7. Heat the oven to 400F.
8. Coat an 8 inch square baking pan with a little olive oil.
9. Trim the ends of the eggplants, then cut eggplants lengthwise into 1/4 inch thick slices.
10. Put non-dairy milk into a bowl and bread crumbs on a plate.
11. Dip each slice into non-dairy milk and then into bread crumbs until each slice is coated lightly in the crumbs.
12. In a large skillet, heat a tablespoon of olive oil on a medium-high heat.

13. Put as many eggplant slices as fit in the skillet and cook until golden brown, turning once, for 2 to 3 minutes per side.
14. Transfer to paper towels to drain, then season lightly with salt and pepper. Repeat with the remaining eggplant.
15. Stir oregano and 1 tablespoon of parsley into the cashew ricotta.
16. Spread one-fourth of tomato sauce on the bottom of the prepared pan, then arrange one-third of eggplant slices on top of the sauce.
17. Sprinkle one-third of basil leaves over the eggplant.
18. Spread one-third of cashew ricotta (about ½ cup) evenly over the basil leaves.
19. Repeat the layers two more times: sauce, eggplant, basil and cashew ricotta.
20. Spread the remaining sauce over the last layer of cashew ricotta.
21. If you have some extra bread-crumbs, you can also sprinkle bread crumbs over the top to give it a crunchy top.
22. Bake for 45 to 60 minutes, until the juices are bubbling. Let stand for 10 minutes before cutting and serving.

Nutritional info (per serving): 530 calories; 31.6 g fat; 52.5 g carbohydrate; 17.6 g protein

Lasagna With Basil Cashew Cheese

Cooking time: 1 hour

Servings: 6

Ingredients:

For the cheese:

- 1 cup raw cashews, soaked in water for 30 minutes or overnight
- 2 garlic cloves, peeled
- 1/4 cup fresh lemon juice
- 1 tablespoon Dijon mustard
- 1/4 cup vegetable broth or water (or more as needed)
- 1.5 cups fresh basil leaves (lightly packed)
- 1/2 cup nutritional yeast (gives the cheese flavour)
- 3/4-1 teaspoon kosher salt (or to taste) + freshly ground black pepper
- 1/2 teaspoon onion powder (optional)

For the lasagna:

- 1 lb box of lasagna noodles
- 1.5 bottles of pasta sauce or use homemade marinara sauce
- 3 garlic cloves, minced
- 1 sweet onion (2.5 cups), chopped

- 2 small zucchini, chopped
- 1 cup cremini mushrooms, sliced
- 1 large red pepper, chopped
- 1 large handful spinach
- 2 pre-cooked veggie burgers, crumbled (optional)
- lemon basil cheese sauce (from above)
- daiya cheese (as much as desired)

Instructions:

1. Drain and rinse soaked cashews. With the food processor turned on, drop in your garlic cloves and process until chopped. Add in the rest of the ingredients and process until smooth, scraping down the bowl as needed.
2. In a large skillet, sauté onion and garlic on a low-medium heat for 5 minutes. Now add the rest of veggies and sauté for another 10-15 minutes. Season well with Herbamare or kosher salt and black pepper.
3. Bring a large pot of water to boil. Boil lasagna noodles for 8 minutes, drain, and rinse immediately with cold water.
4. Add 1 cup pasta sauce on the bottom of your casserole dish. Add a layer of noodles, half of basil cheese sauce, half of vegetables, more pasta sauce, another layer of noodles, veggie burger crumbles (optional), the rest of cheese sauce, the rest of the vegetables, more pasta sauce, and finally a sprinkle of cheese.
5. Preheat the oven to 400F. Cover with tinfoil and prick with fork a few times. Bake at 400F for 40-45 minutes and then remove tinfoil and broil for 5 minutes on medium. Watch closely so you don't burn the edges.

Nutritional info (per serving): 436 calories; 21.5 g fat; 32.4 g carbohydrate; 23 g protein

Lentil Steaks With Mushroom Gravy

Cooking time: 20 minutes

Servings: 4

Ingredients:
- 2 cups lentils, cooked
- ½ cup vegetable broth + 2 cups broth for gravy
- ¼ cup soy sauce
- 1 cup vital wheat gluten
- 1 cup bread crumbs
- ¼ cup liquid smoke
- 2 tablespoons olive oil
- 8 oz mushrooms, sliced
- 3 tablespoons flour
- 2 garlic cloves, minced
- 3 tablespoons vegan butter
- ½ teaspoon dried oregano
- ½ teaspoon dried thyme
- Salt, pepper, to taste

Instructions:
1. Mash cooked lentils with a masher or a fork, in a large bowl. Add wheat gluten, breadcrumbs, ½ cup vegetable broth, soy sauce, liquid smoke, salt and pepper, mix well. Continue to

mix with your hands until well combined. Knead for a few minutes until the mixture forms a dough ball.
2. Separate big balls from the dough and flatter to form steaks.
3. Heat 1 tablespoon oil in a pan over medium heat. Cook steaks for 2-3 minutes on each side. Set cooked steaks aside.
4. Heat 1 more tablespoon oil in a pan. Add mushrooms and garlic. Sauté for 2-3 minutes, add salt and pepper, cook until mushrooms are soft and brown.
5. Reduce heat to low, add flour and butter. Stir for some time, add 2 cups broth. Bring to a boil and let simmer for 2-4 minutes.
6. Serve steaks topped with gravy.

Nutritional info (per serving): 354 calories; 11.5 g fat; 33.6 g carbohydrate; 13 g protein

Vegan Carbonara

Cooking time: 10 minutes

Servings: 4

Ingredients:
- 12 oz spaghetti, uncooked
- 1 tablespoon oil
- 1 onion, chopped
- 2 garlic cloves, minced
- 2 ½ cup almond milk
- ¼ cup flour
- 1 tablespoon nutritional yeast
- 2 teaspoons soy sauce
- ½ cup sundried tomatoes, dry, sliced
- ¼ teaspoon liquid smoke
- Salt, black pepper, to taste

Instructions:
1. Bring a large sauce pan of water to a boil. Add pasta and cook for 8-10 minutes or according to the package instructions.
2. Mix sundried tomatoes, liquid smoke and soy sauce in a bowl and let rest, set aside while you cook the sauce.
3. Preheat oil in a large pan over medium heat. Add onion and garlic, cook for 4-5 minutes.

4. Add flour, whisk for 1 minute and add milk, nutritional yeast, salt and pepper. Cook for 5 minutes. Add more milk if the sauce is too thick.
5. Add sauce and marinated sundried tomatoes to cooked pasta and mix well. Serve and enjoy!

Nutritional info (per serving): 551 calories; 8 g fat; 97 g carbohydrate; 21 g protein

Vegan Tortilla Soup

Cooking time: 20 minutes

Servings: 4

Ingredients:

- 1 can (14 oz) black beans, rinsed and drained
- 1 can (14 oz) hominy, rinsed and drained
- 1 can (14 oz) crushed tomatoes
- 1 dried smoked chili pepper
- 1 tablespoon olive oil
- 1 white onion, diced
- 2 garlic cloves, minced.
- 1 medium jalapeños, deseeded and chopped
- 1 teaspoon ground cumin
- 4 cups vegetable stock
- 6 corn tortillas, sliced into strips
- 1 avocado, diced
- 2 radishes, sliced
- 1 handful cilantro leaves, chopped
- 1 lime, cut into wedges
- Salt, pepper, to taste

Instructions:

1. Preheat the oven to 475 F.

2. Coat a baking sheet with oil. Coat the tortilla strips with oil and arrange them in a single layer. Bake for 6-8 minutes. Season with salt and set aside.
3. Place the dried chili pepper onto a baking sheet and bake for about 1 minute. Open the pepper and remove seeds when cooled down.
4. Preheat some oil in a medium pan over medium heat. Add onion, garlic and jalapeno, cook for 4-5 minutes.
5. Add cumin, tomatoes and vegetable stock. Cook for 3 minutes, add hominy, black beans and toasted chili peppers. Cook for 8-10 minutes. Season with salt and pepper to taste.
6. Once cooked, discard the dried chili pepper. Divide avocado, radishes and tortilla strip among bowls. Top with soup, cilantro leaves and lime wedges.

Nutritional info (per serving): 182 calories; 12 g fat; 17 g carbohydrate; 2 g protein

Mushroom Bean Avocado Toast

Cooking time: 5 minutes

Servings: 2

Ingredients:

- 1 avocado, mashed
- 1 tablespoon (14 ml) lemon juice
- 1 tablespoon (14 ml) oil
- 4 oz (113 g) mushrooms
- ½ cup (64 g) cooked cannellini beans
- 1 oz (28 g) microgreens
- 1 tablespoon (14 g) miso paste
- 1 tablespoon (14 ml) balsamic vinegar
- 4 slices whole grain bread, toasted
- 1 tablespoon (14 g) sesame seeds, for serving

Instructions:

1. Mix avocado and lemon juice in a bowl. Set aside.
2. Preheat oil in a pan over medium heat. Add mushrooms and cook for 5 minutes. Add beans and microgreens and turn off the heat.
3. Mix miso paste and 1 tablespoon water in a bowl. Add to mushrooms and beans, mix to combine. Add vinegar and set aside.

4. Spread avocado on each bread slice. Spoon mushroom mixture on top. Top with sesame seeds and serve.

Nutritional info (per serving): 581 calories; 29.5 g fat; 65.6 g carbohydrate; 21.6 g protein

Roasted Cauliflowers With Tomato Sauce

Cooking time: 30 minutes

Servings: 4

Ingredients:

- 1 tablespoon olive oil
- 1 onion, chopped
- 2 carrots, chopped
- 1 cup mushrooms, chopped
- 2 cups tomato sauce
- 1 tablespoon vegan Worcestershire sauce
- 4 small whole cauliflowers
- ½ cup baby spinach
- ½ cup vegan cheese, shredded

Instructions:

1. Put olive oil into a sauté pan and heat it. Then add onion, carrot and mushrooms and cook for 10 minutes.
2. Add tomato paste and vegan Worcestershire sauce, and simmer for 10 minutes.
3. Put cauliflowers into the microwave and cook for about 5 minutes to soften.
4. Put spinach on the bottom of an ovenproof dish. Top with cauliflowers and pour over the vegetable sauce.

5. Preheat the oven to 375F, cover with foil and bake for 10 minutes. Later top with vegand cheese, put back into the oven for 5 minutes to melt the cheese.

Nutritional info (per serving): 407 calories; 22 g fat; 9 g carbohydrate; 19 g protein

Tofu Cashew Coconut Curry

Cooking time: 30 minutes

Servings: 4

Ingredients:

- 1 package extra firm tofu, drained, cubed
- 1 sweet potato, diced
- ½ cauliflower head, broken into florets, chopped
- 1 jalapeño, diced
- 1 bell pepper, diced
- 2 carrots, chopped
- 3 garlic cloves, minced
- 1 tablespoon virgin coconut oil
- 1 tablespoon fresh ginger, grated
- 2 tablespoons curry powder
- ½ teaspoon turmeric
- ½ teaspoon cumin
- ¼ teaspoon ground cinnamon
- 1 can (14 oz) light coconut milk
- 1 cup tomato sauce
- 1 cup vegetarian broth
- 3 tablespoons roasted cashews, ground
- Salt, to taste
- Fresh cilantro, chopped, for serving

Instructions:

1. Preheat oil in a pot over medium heat. Add garlic, ginger, potato, jalapeno, bell pepper, carrots and cauliflower. Cook for 10 minutes stirring often.
2. Add curry powder, turmeric, cumin, cinnamon and salt. Add coconut milk, tomato sauce, broth and cashews. Stir well until combined.
3. Add tofu, stir once again. Cook on low heat for 20 minutes. Serve topped with cilantro.

Nutritional info (per serving): 342 calories; 20.4 g fat; 26.2 g carbohydrate; 14.1 g protein

Vegan Frittata

Cooking time: 45 minutes

Servings: 6

Ingredients:
- 1 ½ cup chickpea flour
- 1 ½ cup water
- ¼ cup plain vegan yogurt
- 1 tablespoon oil
- ½ cup fresh cilantro, chopped
- ½ teaspoon ground turmeric
- ¼ teaspoon dried thyme
- 2 cups broccoli flowers, chopped
- 1 onion, chopped
- ½ cup frozen peas
- Salt, pepper, to taste

Instructions:
1. Mix flour, water, yogurt, oil, turmeric, thyme and salt in a bowl or use a blender to mix well.
2. Preheat oven to 375F. Line a baking dish (9 inch) with a parchment paper.
3. Add broccoli, onion, peas and cilantro to frittata batter and pour it all into a baking dish. Cook for 45-50 minutes. Let cool a little before serving.

Nutritional info (per serving): 211 calories; 10.6 g fat; 23.8 g carbohydrate; 7.7 g protein

Spinach Ravioli

Cooking time: 10 minutes

Servings: 4

Ingredients:

- 1 package (12 oz) vegan wonton wrappers
- 8 oz spinach, frozen
- 1 cup vegan ricotta
- ¼ cup fresh basil, chopped
- 3-4 cups water
- Salt, pepper, to taste

Instructions:

1. Mix basil, ricotta, spinach, salt and pepper in a bowl.
2. Place wrappers on a counter. Put about 1 tablespoon filling in the center of each wrapper, put another wrapper on top and press down with your fingers to seal. Repeat with the rest of wrappers.
3. Bring water to a boil in a sauce pan. Add ravioli and cook for 2-3 minutes. Serve hot topped with some more fresh basil.

Nutritional info (per serving): 171 calories; 1.4 g fat; 23.9 g carbohydrate; 13.7 g protein

Peanut Noodles

Cooking time: 10 minutes

Servings: 4

Ingredients:

- ½ package rice noodles
- 3 tablespoons peanut butter
- ¼ cup soy sauce
- 3 green onions, chopped
- 1 tablespoon apple cider vinegar
- 1 tablespoon Hoisin sauce
- ¼ teaspoon ground ginger
- 1 package frozen veggies of choice
- ¼ cup water
- 2 garlic cloves, minced

Instructions:

1. Prepare a large pan. Add all the ingredients except for noodles and vegetables to a pan. Heat over medium heat until bubbly and turn off the heat, stir well.
2. Bring a medium sauce pan of water to a boil and turn off the heat. Add noodles and frozen vegetables, let stay for 10 minutes and drain.

3. Serve veggies and noodles with sauce on top.

Nutritional info (per serving): 540 calories; 26 g fat; 60 g carbohydrate; 19 g protein

Creamy Vegan Pasta

Cooking time: 18 minutes

Servings: 3

Ingredients:

- 1 onion, chopped
- 2 cloves garlic, minced
- 1 zucchini, chopped
- 1 small red bell pepper, chopped
- 4.5 cups uncooked fusilli
- 1.5 teaspoons red curry paste
- 3 cups diced tomatoes, canned (do not drain)
- 1 cup canned coconut milk (whole fat) (use the creamy part)
- 1/2 cup frozen peas
- 1/2 cup cherry tomatoes, cut into halves
- salt, to taste
- black pepper, to taste
- 1 teaspoon fresh lemon juice

Instructions:

1. Heat some oil in a large pot and sauté onion for about 2-3 minutes. Then add garlic, zucchini, red bell pepper and cook for 2 more minutes.

2. Add the remaining ingredients except for the cherry tomatoes. Cook for about 15 minutes uncovered and on a medium heat.
3. Then add cherry tomatoes and cook for 2 more minutes. Season with salt and black pepper.

Nutritional info (per serving): 529 calories; 19 g fat; 79 g carbohydrate; 19 g protein

Taco Pizza

Cooking time: 10 minutes

Servings: 3

Ingredients:

- 1 cup walnuts
- 1 cup brown lentils
- 1 tablespoon olive oil
- 1/2 onion
- 1 tablespoon tomato paste
- 1/2 cup diced tomatoes
- 1 teaspoon cumin
- 1 teaspoon paprika powder
- 2 teaspoons oregano
- salt, to taste
- black pepper, to taste
- 1 pre-made pizza dough
- 1 cup vegan sour cream
- 1 avocado, cut into pieces
- 2 tomatoes, cut into pieces
- 2 cups lettuce, cut into stripes
- 1/2 cup kidney beans
- 1/2 cup corn
- 1/2 cup vegan cheese

- red pepper flakes (optional)

Instructions:

1. Cook lentils according to the instructions. Drain and set aside.
2. In a medium pan, roast walnuts without oil for about 2 minutes or until they're lightly golden.
3. Put walnuts and cooked lentils into a food processor and process until chopped.
4. In a medium pan, heat olive oil on a medium heat and sauté onions for about 3 minutes.
5. Add lentil walnut mixture and stir in the tomato paste and cook for 2 minutes.
6. Add diced tomatoes and spices (paprika powder, cumin, oregano) and season with salt and pepper.
7. Preheat the oven to 385F and bake the pizza dough for about 10 minutes until it's golden and crispy.
8. After baking, evenly spread pizza with vegan sour cream.
9. Add a layer of vegan lentil walnut meat and top with avocado, tomatoes, lettuce, corn, kidney beans, and vegan cheese.
10. Sprinkle with red pepper flakes.

Nutritional info (per serving): 364 calories; 14 g fat; 47 g carbohydrate; 12 g protein

Vegan Chili Cheese Fries

Cooking time: 15 minutes

Servings: 2

Ingredients:

For the vegan chili:

- 1.25 cups canned kidney beans
- 1.5 cups canned black beans
- 3/4 cup canned corn
- 2 cloves of garlic, minced
- 1 onion, chopped
- 1 teaspoon paprika powder
- 1 teaspoon chili powder
- 2 tablespoons tomato paste
- 1 teaspoon cumin
- 1/4 teaspoon liquid smoke (optional)
- 1 tablespoon oregano
- salt, to taste
- black pepper, to taste
- 1 14 oz can diced tomatoes

For the fries:

- 3 large potatoes

- salt, to taste
- 1 tablespoon olive oil

For the cheese sauce:

- 1/2 cup cashews
- 1 clove of garlic
- 1 teaspoon white miso paste
- 1/2 heaped cup white beans
- 1/2 cup nutritional yeast
- 1/4 cup unsweetened plant-based milk (preferably soy, almond, or oat)
- 1/2 teaspoon paprika powder
- salt, to taste
- black pepper, to taste

Additional ingredients:

- green onions and fresh cilantro, to serve
- black olives, cut into rings
- fresh cilantro

Instructions:

1. Preheat the oven to 350F. Cut potatoes into French fries and bake for about 30 minutes until crispy.
2. Heat some oil in a large pan and sauté onion for about 2 minutes.
3. Then add garlic and cook it for 1 more minute.
4. Add the tomato paste, chili and paprika powder, and cook for 2 minutes.
5. Now add liquid smoke (if using), cumin, diced tomatoes, oregano, kidney beans, black beans, and the corn. Simmer for 10 minutes.
6. To make the vegan cheese sauce, combine all ingredients in a high speed blender and blend until smooth and creamy.

7. Once fries are ready, add chili and cheese on top and bake for another 10 minutes.
8. Serve with green onions, fresh cilantro, and black onions.

Nutritional info (per serving): 402 calories; 1.7 g fat; 88 g carbohydrate; 14.9 g protein

Saucy Meatballs With Spaghetti

Cooking time: 30 minutes

Servings: 4

Ingredients:

For the vegan meatballs:

- 1 15 oz can kidney beans
- 1/2 tablespoon olive oil
- 1 large clove of garlic, minced
- 1/2 onion, chopped
- 1 teaspoon oregano
- 1 teaspoon basil
- 1 tablespoon tomato paste
- 1 teaspoon soy sauce
- 1/2 cup rolled oats
- 1/3 heaped cup sunflower seeds
- salt
- black pepper

For the chunky marinara sauce:

- 1/2 tablespoon olive oil
- 1 small onion, chopped
- 1 large clove garlic, minced

- 1 carrot, cut into small pieces
- 1 tablespoon tomato paste
- 1/4 cup dry red wine
- 1 can diced tomatoes (14,5 oz)
- 1 teaspoon oregano
- fresh basil leaves, cut into small pieces
- salt
- black pepper
- For the spaghetti:
- 9 oz whole wheat spaghetti

For the cashew Parmesan:

- 1/2 cup unsalted cashews
- 2 tablespoons nutritional yeast
- 1/4 teaspoon garlic powder
- salt

Instructions:

1. Cook the spaghetti according to the instructions on the package.
2. Rinse and drain the kidney beans. Put them in a medium bowl and mash them well with a fork or a potato masher.
3. In a medium pan, heat some oil and sauté the onions for 3 minutes. Add the minced garlic and cook for another minute.
4. Put the sunflower seeds in a food processor and pulse until a fine meal is achieved.
5. Add the sauteed onion and garlic to the mashed beans together with the spices, the tomato paste, the soy sauce, the ground sunflower seeds, and the oats. Season with salt and pepper.
6. Use your hands to thoroughly mix everything. Then form about 12-14 vegan meatballs. (Please note that I doubled the recipe for the photos, so there are more meatballs).

7. Preheat the oven to 350F and bake the vegan meatballs for about 15 minutes. Carefully flip them halfway through the baking time.
8. Alternatively you could also pan-fry them. In a medium pan, heat some olive oil over medium heat and gently roast the bean balls for about 4 minutes until they are golden. You'll achieve the best results with a cast iron pan. However, I would recommend the baking version. Not only is this version oil-free, they meatballs also become more crispier and firmer this way.
9. Make the marinara sauce: In a medium pan, heat the olive oil over medium heat. Sauté the onions for 3 minutes, then add the garlic and the carrot. Cook for another 2-3 minutes. Stir in the tomato paste and cook for 2 minutes.
10. Then deglaze with red wine and allow to evaporate. Add diced tomatoes and simmer for about 10 minutes. Season with oregano, salt, and pepper. Before serving add some fresh basil leaves.
11. Make the cashew Parmesan: Put the cashews, nutritional yeast, salt, and garlic powder in a food processor and pulse until a fine meal is achieved.
12. Serve the spaghetti with the marinara and vegan meatballs and sprinkle with Parmesan and fresh basil leaves.

Nutritional info (per serving): 459 calories; 12 g fat; 73 g carbohydrate; 17 g protein

Chickpea Curry With Potatoes

Cooking time: 25 minutes

Servings: 3

Ingredients:

- Jasmine rice
- 1 small onion, cut into stripes
- 2 small potatoes, cut into small pieces
- 1 large carrot, cut into slices
- 1 teaspoon curry powder
- 1 teaspoon red curry paste (optional) adjust if the curry paste you're using is very spicy, mine was very mild
- 1 cup full fat coconut milk
- 1/2 cup vegetable broth
- 1 1/2 cups cooked chickpeas
- 1 cup frozen peas
- salt
- black pepper
- cashews (optional)
- fresh cilantro (optional)

Instructions:

1. Cook the Jasmine rice according to the instructions on the package.

2. In a large pan, heat some oil and sauté the onion for 2-3 minutes. Then add the potatoes and cook for another 3 minutes. Stir in the red curry paste and the curry and cook for another minute.
3. Add the coconut milk, vegetable broth, carrot, chickpeas, and peas and cook for about 20 minutes.
4. Season with salt and pepper and serve with cashews and cilantro.

Nutritional info (per serving): 404 calories; 21 g fat; 46 g carbohydrate; 12 g protein

Classic Vegan Coleslaw

Cooking time: 10 minutes

Servings: 8

Ingredients:

- 1 small head green cabbage (about 6 – 7 cups), shredded
- 1/2 small red cabbage (about 3 cups), shredded
- 1.5 cups carrots, shredded or julienned
- 2/3 cup vegan mayonnaise
- 1 tablespoon Dijon mustard
- 2 tablespoons apple cider vinegar
- 1-2 teaspoons pure cane sugar
- salt & pepper, to taste

Instructions:

1. To make the dressing, whisk the mayonnaise in a small bowl,, apple cider vinegar, mustard, sugar, salt, and pepper.
2. Put cabbage and carrots into a very large mixing bowl, the larger the better. Pour the dressing all over the cabbage, and toss well to combine.
3. Serve right away, or let the coleslaw rest in the fridge for at least 30 minutes before serving.
4. Store leftovers in the refrigerator in an airtight container for up to 5 days, but it's best within 3 days.

Nutritional info (per serving): 116 calories; 6.9 g fat; 11.6 g carbohydrate; 3.4 g protein

Herbed Potato, Asparagus And Chickpeas

Cooking time: 40 minutes

Servings: 3

Ingredients:

- 1 lb baby red potatoes, sliced in half lengthwise
- 1.5 cups petite baby carrots
- 1 can (14oz.) chickpeas, drained and rinsed
- 1 teaspoon of each dried basil, dried thyme, dried oregano (see notes)
- 1 teaspoon paprika
- 1/2 teaspoon garlic powder
- 2-3 tablespoons olive oil, divided
- 1 lb asparagus, ends trimmed and cut into thirds
- 1/2 large yellow onion, sliced lengthwise
- mineral salt & fresh cracked pepper, to taste
- fresh parsley, to serve

Instructions:

1. Preheat oven to 425 . Line a rimmed baking sheet with parchment paper, silpat or lightly grease with oil.
2. Add the potatoes, carrots and chickpeas to the sheet pan, drizzle with 1 1/2 tablespoon olive oil and 3/4 of the spices, toss to coat. Arrange the potatoes flesh side down, this will

help them get crispy edges. Place in the oven for 20 -25 minutes.
3. Carefully remove the pan from the oven, push the potato mixture to one side, add the onion and asparagus, add the remaining oil and herb/spice mix, toss to coat. Place sheet pan back in the oven and roast for 10 – 15 minutes more.
4. Let cool a few minutes. Serve with parsley sprinkled over top and sliced avocado on the side. Would be great with a serving of quinoa on the side as well, adding more fiber and protein!
5. Store leftovers in an airtight container in the refrigerator for up to 5 – 6 days.

Nutritional info (per serving): 356 calories; 9.6 g fat; 58.6 g carbohydrate; 11.8 g protein

Banana Chia Pudding

Cooking time: 6 hours

Servings: 4

Ingredients:

- 2 large overripe bananas
- 2 cups unsweetened coconut (beverage), almond or cashew milk
- 6 tablespoons chia seeds

Optional add-ins:

- 2–4 tablespoons pure maple syrup
- 1/2–1 teaspoon vanilla extract

To garnish:

- toasted coconut flakes
- banana slices
- cacao nibs or shaved dark chocolate

Instructions:

1. In a medium bowl, add bananas and mash well, stir in non-dairy milk and chia seeds, mix well.
2. Let set for about 30 minutes, and give a good stir, repeat one more time, stirring again after 30 minutes. This step is an important step, as the seeds need to be stirred once or twice before completely gelling up and setting. If not stirred, the

mixture will be soupy. Cover and place in the refrigerator for at least 6 hours, or overnight.
3. Serve with sliced bananas, toasted coconut flakes and cacao nibs/shaved chocolate. Would also be great with a dollop of coconut whipped cream!

Nutritional info (per serving): 175 calories; 7.7 g fat; 24.5 g carbohydrate; 4.7 g protein

Creamy Broccoli Cheese Soup

Cooking time: 30 minutes

Servings: 6-8

Ingredients:

- 1 tablespoon extra-virgin olive oil
- 1 large yellow onion, finely diced (about 1 1/2 cups)
- 1 medium shallot, minced
- 1 teaspoon smoked paprika
- 2 teaspoons sea salt, divided, plus more to taste
- freshly ground black pepper, to taste
- 4 small or 2 large heads broccoli, destemmed, and chopped into small 1/2-inch florets (1 lb florets or 5-6 cups)
- 4 cups low-sodium vegetable broth, divided
- 2 cups filtered water
- 2 cups small cauliflower florets
- 1/2 cup shelled hemp seeds
- 1/2 cup chopped roasted and peeled red peppers
- 1/2 cup nutritional yeast
- 1 tablespoon arrowroot powder
- 1 tablespoon apple cider vinegar
- 1 tablespoon fresh lemon juice
- 1 tablespoon reduced-sodium tamari

Instructions:

1. Heat olive oil in a large Dutch oven or stock pot on a medium-low heat.
2. Add onion, shallot, smoked paprika, 1 teaspoon sea salt, black pepper, and cook for 6 minutes stirring occasionally or until the onion is soft and translucent.
3. Add broccoli florets, 3 cups vegetable broth, filtered water, increase the heat to a medium-high and bring to a rapid simmer for 5 minutes. Reduce the heat to medium-low, cover, and simmer for 20 to 25 minutes or until broccoli florets are fork-tender, stirring occasionally to ensure that the broccoli is submerged.
4. Bring a medium pot of water to a boil. Put cauliflower florets into the pot and boil for 7 minutes or until very fork-tender. Strain off water.
5. Add boiled cauliflower florets, remaining 1 cup vegetable broth, hemp hearts, roasted red peppers, nutritional yeast, arrowroot powder, apple cider vinegar, and the remaining 1 teaspoon sea salt to a high-speed blender. Blend on high for 2 minutes or until completely smooth and creamy.
6. Once the broccoli florets are fork-tender, pour cauliflower "cheddar" sauce into the pot and stir to combine.
7. Increase the heat to medium and continue stirring for 3-5 minutes or until the soup begins to thicken.
8. Once the soup has thickened slightly, remove from the heat and stir in the fresh lemon juice and tamari.
9. Taste and season with more sea salt, black pepper, and smoked paprika, if desired.

Nutritional info (per serving): 249 calories; 13 g fat; 12 g carbohydrate; 13 g protein

Grilled Cheese With Smoky Tomato Soup

Cooking time: 45 minutes

Servings: 4

Ingredients:

For the cheese:

- 1/2 can full-fat coconut milk (6.83 fl. oz.)
- 1/2 teaspoon coconut vinegar
- 1/2 teaspoon salt
- 1 teaspoon agar powder
- 1/2 tablespoon tapioca flour
- 1 tablespoon nooch

For the soup:

- 1 tablespoon olive oil
- 1 small onion, chopped
- 4 garlic cloves, smashed
- 1/2 teaspoon dried thyme
- 1/2 teaspoon dried basil
- 1/2 teaspoon dried oregano
- few dashes liquid smoke
- 1 cup prepared crushed roma tomatoes

- 2 cups homemade stock

For the sandwich:

- 4 pieces sandwich bread
- vegan butter, softened at room temperature

Instructions:

To make the cheese
1. Combine all of cheese ingredients (except the nooch) in a small saucepan.
2. Whisk briskly continuously until the mixture comes to a boil.
3. Remove it from the heat, stir in nooch and transfer it to a small pyrex dish.
4. Cover and chill in the refrigerator for at least 1 hour.

To make the soup
5. Heat oil in a medium-sized saucepan on a medium heat, add onions and sauté for about 7 minutes until translucent and slightly browned.
6. Reduce the heat to a medium low, add garlic, spices, liquid smoke and allow to sauté for about 3 minutes, stirring occassionally.
7. Now add prepared roma tomatoes and vegan broth. Return the heat to medium until soup comes to a very small boil. Then dial the heat back down to low and allow to simmer for about 15 minutes.
8. At this point, you can remove soup from the heat and blend it well with an immersion blender.

To make the sandwiches
9. Put 1/2 tablespoon vegan butter into a skillet on a medium heat.
10. Spread one of the slices of bread with a thin layer of cheese, then place bread piece cheese side up on the skillet.
11. Swirl it around to ensure it gets coated well with the vegan butter.

12. Spread the other slice of bread with softened butter and put it butter side up on top.
13. Allow bread to nicely brown for about 4 minutes on one side before flipping it over with a spatula.
14. Sprinkle with a little salt on top if desired.

Nutritional info (per serving): 71 calories; 4 g fat; 7 g carbohydrate; 1 g protein

French Dip Sandwiches

Cooking time: 35 minutes

Servings: 2

Ingredients:

- 2 tablespoons olive oil, divided
- 1 medium onion, sliced into half rings
- 2 garlic cloves, minced
- 3 portobello mushroom caps, (about 20 oz total), cleaned and sliced into thin strips
- 1 cup vegetable broth
- 1 tablespoon soy sauce
- 1 tablespoon vegan Worcestershire sauce
- 1/2 teaspoon dried thyme

- 1/4 teaspoon liquid smoke, (optional, but highly recommended)
- 1/4 teaspoon black pepper
- 2-6 inch sandwich rolls or baguette sections sliced open
- horseradish mustard

Instructions:

1. Coat the bottom of a large skillet with 1 tablespoon oil and place over medium-low heat.
2. Add onion and toss a few times to coat with oil. Allow to cook until caramelized, for about 20 minutes, flipping occasionally.
3. Add garlic and cook for about 2 minutes more. Transfer onions and garlic to a plate.
4. Coat skillet with another tablespoon of oil and raise heat to medium. Add mushroom strips, avoid overcrowding the skillet.
5. Cook until lightly browned, for about 5 minutes. Flip and cook 5 minutes more on the opposite sides.
6. Return onions to the skillet, add broth, soy sauce, Worchestershire sauce, thyme, liquid smoke, pepper and bring to a simmer and allow to cook, stirring occasionally, until liquid is reduced by half, for about 5 minutes.
7. Slather the insides of rolls with horseradish mustard.
8. Use a slotted spoon to remove onions and mushrooms from skillet, pressing lightly to squeeze out any excess juice.
9. Divide onions and mushrooms into rolls.
10. Pour cooking liquid into a small bowl and serve with sandwiches, for dipping.

Nutritional info (per serving): 436 calories; 20 g fat; 48 g carbohydrate; 7 g protein